# THE FIRST PRICE GUIDE TO ANTIQUE AND VINTAGE CLOTHES

# THE FIRST PRICE GUIDE TO ANTIQUE AND VINTAGE CLOTHES

## Fashions for Women
## 1840–1940

### TINA IRICK-NAUER

Photographs by John J. Nauer

E.P. DUTTON, INC.   NEW YORK

Copyright © 1983 by Tina Irick-Nauer

All rights reserved. Printed in the U.S.A.

No part of this publication may be reproduced or transmitted in any form or by any means, electronic or mechanical, including photocopy, recording or any information storage and retrieval system now known or to be invented, without permission in writing from the publisher, except by a reviewer who wishes to quote brief passages in connection with a review written for inclusion in a magazine, newspaper or broadcast.

Published in the United States by
E. P. Dutton, Inc., 2 Park Avenue,
New York, N.Y. 10016

Library of Congress Catalog Card Number: 82-46045

Designed by Stanley S. Drate

ISBN: 0-525-48050-1

Published simultaneously in Canada by
Clarke, Irwin & Company Limited, Toronto and Vancouver
W

10 9 8 7 6 5 4 3 2 1

First Edition

Color insert printed by South China Printing Co., Hong Kong.

# CONTENTS

ACKNOWLEDGMENTS
page 7

INTRODUCTION
page 9

**1840–1850**
page 11

**1851–1860**
page 19

**1861–1870**
page 27

**1871–1880**
page 33

**1881–1890**
page 43

**1891–1900**
page 53

**1901–1910**
page 67

**1911–1920**
page 81

**1921–1930**
page 95

**1931–1940**
page 109

THE CARE AND CLEANING OF ANTIQUE CLOTHES
page 125

SOURCES FOR ANTIQUE CLOTHES
page 127

*Color insert follows page 64*

# ACKNOWLEDGMENTS

I SHOULD LIKE to thank all my friends and my dear family for their support and encouragement. They gave up a great deal of their time with me so that I could write this book. I extend deep appreciation to my husband, John, for all his work on the photography. Adrienne St. Pierre at AITA was an important link to the past with her fine costume identification course. Many shops and private collections made their clothing available, and their help and hospitality are appreciated. I should especially like to thank Theron Ware and the docents of the Campbell House Museum in St. Louis.

My most heartfelt thanks go to Betty Demeo, without whom this book could not have been written.

# INTRODUCTION

THE JOY AND fantasy of collecting and wearing antique and vintage clothes has spread rapidly across the United States and Europe over the last ten years. Thus it is time for a price guide to be published so both buyers and sellers may evaluate these fine things properly. I have collected antique clothes for twenty years, from the time when you could purchase a white tea dress dating from around 1900 for only $10.00. *Those* days are certainly gone forever! I also sell antique clothes at Laughing Cat Antiques in Houston, Texas, and I wanted to write this book to show some of these beauties in print and to help standardize prices.

The objects and the prices published here have been gathered from shops across the United States over a six-month period. Over 300 data sheets and requests for information were mailed out. The shops that chose to participate in this project are listed as sources at the back of the book. In addition, my husband, John (who did the photography), and I traveled to six major cities making photographs and gathering data. We are most grateful to have been allowed to see and photograph pieces in some wonderful private and museum collections. As I am an avid collector, this part of working on the book was a magnificent experience.

The prices published here vary according to the age and condition of the garment. Prices on the East and West coasts are slightly higher for certain kinds of clothing than are the prices found for similar pieces in the South and the Midwest. Naturally, prices will be higher for pieces that are rare, for couturier-designed pieces, and for garments made of special fabric or having special trim. Also, a price will often be higher than usual if the dealer can prove that the garment had once belonged to a famous personality.

Sizes are not specifically given in the guide, but as a rule of thumb clothing of the period 1840 to 1900 will be quite small, often as small as size 1 or size 3. The smallness of the clothing is a result of both the heavy corseting that was then the rule and the fact that women of that time were physically smaller. After about 1900 the sizes tend to become more wearable.

I also wish to say something about making repairs and size changes in the garments. Antique clothing is considerably lessened in value for collectors when radical additions or subtractions have been made. If any repairs or changes are to be done, they should be done with materials from the period or as close as possible to the original period of the garment. An appropriate example would be the case of a typical Victorian batiste blouse or waist. Invariably, these pieces are too short in the back to tuck into skirts or pants. It would be acceptable, therefore, to find some matching batiste of the period and sew on a three-inch peplum that can be tucked into a skirt. It would be unacceptable to use a polyester fabric for the same purpose.

There is a major difference to be found between a collector and/or restorer and a consumer. The consumer will wear and enjoy clothing. Considering that the whole point is to make the antique garment wearable, the consumer might, for example, replace mother-of-pearl buttons with ones made of plastic that resemble mother-of-pearl. The collector or museum curator, however, would much prefer that all parts of the garment be original to the period of its creation even if the garment is in disrepair, or would be willing to wait until one could find mother-of-pearl buttons that match the originals exactly. Both of these antique-clothes enthusiasts have a valid point of view, and one can be both of these people. I have pieces in my collection that I have never put on because they are too old or precious to subject to stress. On the other hand, I own other pieces that I wear two or three times a week and to almost all formal or party occasions.

Clothing, particularly women's clothing, makes such a marvelous commentary on the social, religious, economic, and sexual mores of the times that I find studying the clothes completely fascinating. They are part of an ongoing history that is really a world unto itself. Thus, when I am asked why I want to own old clothes or why I love to wear them, I am able to reply that they have put me into the mainstream of social history and that they have greatly broadened my knowledge of the world and have thus greatly enriched my fantasy life.

# 1840–1850

MANY GARMENTS of the 1840 period were remodeled from dresses of the 1780s, for skirts of the earlier period were so huge. Clothing was mostly handmade and very expensive. Most women had only two or three dresses. The sewing machine was used primarily for making shoes, but some clothing had machine stitching. Skirts were designed to be open in the front with decoration in the open areas. The waist was sewn down, not cut off and bound. The favorite colors were browns, greens, and some lavender. Fine embroidered muslin imported from India was popular. The best dresses were made of ivory damask. Decoration on clothing usually consisted of quilting or cording. Wood buttons were also used as decoration, not for closure. The ideal silhouette was long-waisted and slope-shouldered.

Skirts were full and dome-shaped with the help of at least six petticoats. Empress Josephine of France made fine white batiste underwear with elaborate decoration popular. By 1850 hoops had replaced petticoats. Most dresses of this time had small cord piping sewn in at every seam. The hooks and eyes were much larger than what we are used to now and were made of copper or brass. Aprons and other detachable accessories such as collars were prevalent. Torsos were enclosed in long-sleeved, boned bodices over tightly laced corsets with a V-shaped decoration emphasizing a long waist. Sleeves were very tight with some fullness at the wrist.

Because women were much smaller, heavily corseted, and did very little physically, the clothing from 1840 to 1850 is very tight and constricted. Many of the available pieces are in good to excellent shape, but not really wearable because of size and construction. These dresses are usually collected only for historical reasons and if worn, would be consumed shortly. More examples of the underwear, aprons, and accessories have survived from this period and are very wearable.

# OUTERWEAR

1842—Black polished-cotton top and skirt; bodice is printed with lavender-colored violets and has black lace at neck; bustle back; *Excellent*; $150.

1845—Small black-and-white print blouse; black skirt and wool cape; typical of the clothes worn on the American frontier; *Fine*; $175.

1845—White cotton-voile dress printed with a ribbon motif decorated with pastel flowers; full sleeves have lace trim, and there is a flounce at the hem; front closure; Author's Collection; *Excellent*; $300; *Not for sale.*

---

1849—White cotton-voile skirt with small brown flower print; ruffle on bottom; *Fair*; $35.

# UNDERWEAR

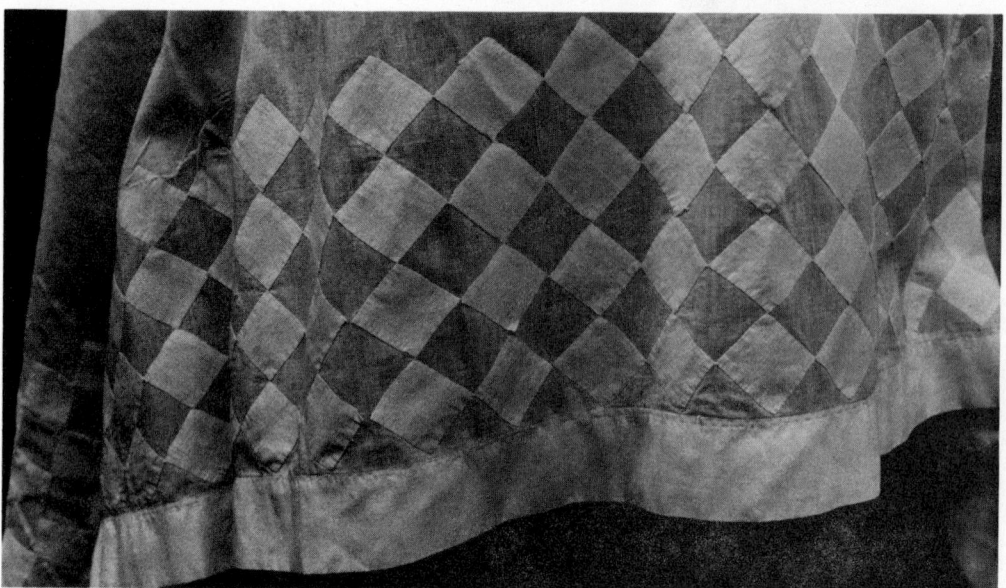

1840—Detail of patchwork on an unusual homespun petticoat; courtesy Frances Altman, Atlanta; *Mint*; $120.

1843—White cotton nightgown with tucks extending down full front and back; open-front placket to waist and full-length open back placket; handmade eyelet lace on cuffs and placket; *Excellent*; $175.

1845—One-piece white cotton underwear with button crotch and drawstring waist; *Good*; $8.

1849—White cotton nightgown; hand-embroidered with a butterfly motif and intertwining ribbons; wide sleeves; *F* monogram; *Excellent*; $95.

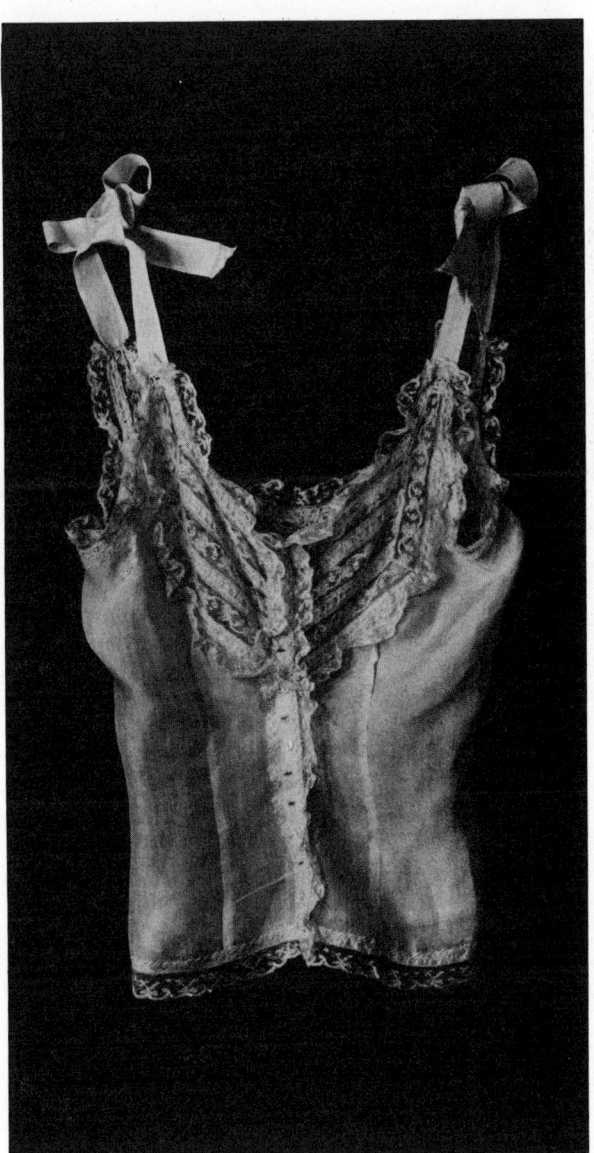

1850—Ecru silk bodice with handmade lace insert and trim; profuse ribbons and embroidery; courtesy Laughing Cat Antiques, Houston; *Mint*; $85.

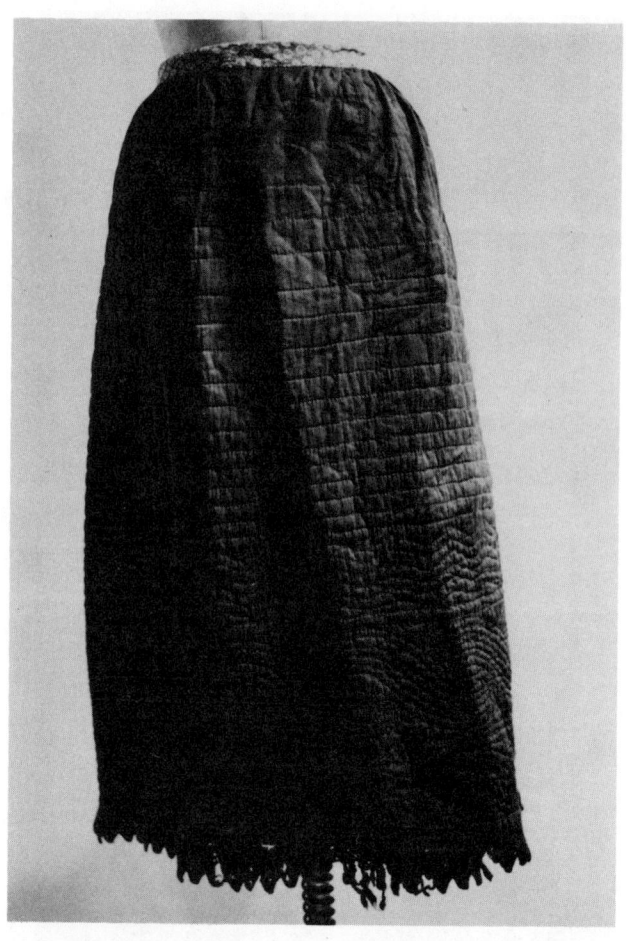

1850—Black hand-quilted cotton petticoat with crocheted hem; drawstring waistband; courtesy FDR Drive, New York City; *Excellent*; $125.

1850—Heavy white cotton petticoat with ruching and lots of tucking; fitted yoke and hip with slight train; courtesy Laughing Cat Antiques, Houston; *Excellent*; $90.

# HATS, PURSES, SHOES, AND ACCESSORIES

1840—Blue wide-brim hat with chiffon flowers; *Mint–Excellent*; $65.

1840—Gobelin-type tapestry purse with swan clasp and bouquet closure in brass; chain strap; *Excellent*; $75.

1843—Nightcap of white handmade lace; *Mint*; $35.

1843—Wine felt hat with crushed wine velvet and feathers in red and black; *Mint*; $75.

1845—Gray French silk purse with gray silk rope handle and pewter rope design and clasp ending in filigree balls; *Mint*; $65.

1850—Woven-straw poke bonnet with blue-and-white calico print; *Mint*; $50.

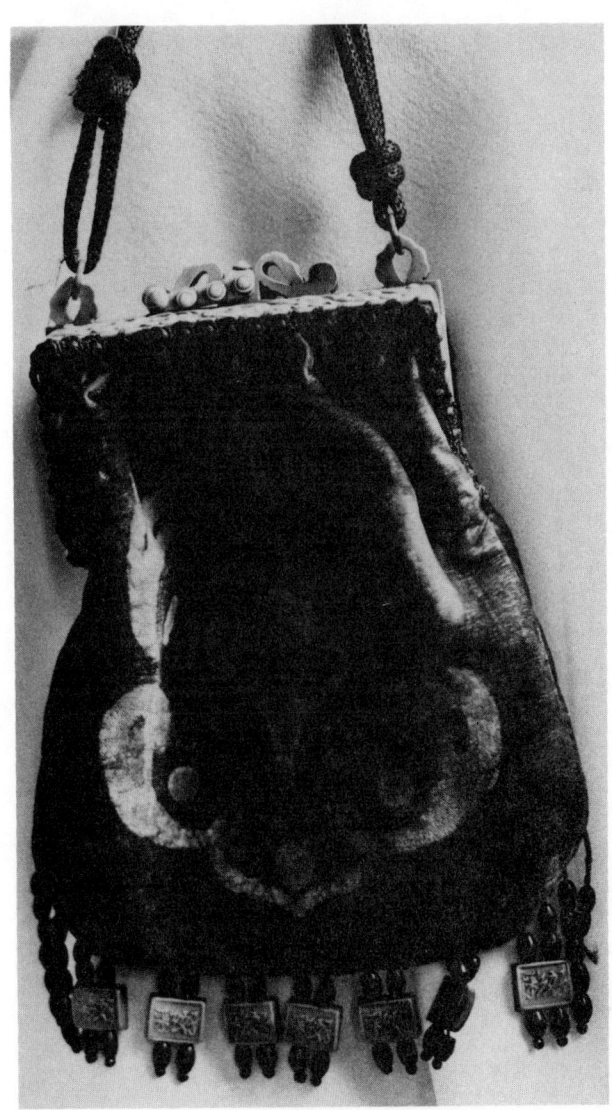

1850—Cut-velvet-type bag in dull green, blue, and red with ornate German silver clasp; courtesy Early Halloween, New York City; *Excellent*; $55.

# 1851–1860

By 1850 six rollers were used in fabric printing and favorite colors were lavender, peacock, fawn, or stone. The sewing machine made "ready-to-wear" clothing possible in the mid-1850s. The invention of aniline color-fast dyes provided more color contrast. Many fabrics, such as brocade, satin, and velvet, were woven and used in combination with plain fabrics. New fabrics were challis and nainsook.

The trimmings of the time became more elaborate with ball fringes, tassels, buttons, and lace made of chenille. The hat was a small straw bonnet. Caps were still worn indoors by ladies. Accessories included striped stockings, aprons, short embroidered gloves, small parasols, and dotted-swiss hairnets. The silhouette was slightly more relaxed as corseting became less rigid and the long bodices shortened. Buttons were now used for fastening.

Skirts became rounder and fuller. Empress Eugénie of France made hoopskirts fashionable, and they reached their ultimate fullness at the close of 1850. Double skirts, three-tiered skirts, or mantles, and jackets that reached the hip gave the multiple-skirt illusion. Skirt ruffles multiplied, and the hem normally had a wide, pleated flounce.

Sleeves spread into wide pagoda forms, and the use of a detachable sleeve, or *engageante,* was popular. Necklines were high with small white collars. Back lacing started in this decade and was prevalent in 1860. Capes and mantles became very fashionable. Occasionally, separates began to be seen. The great French couturier Worth was dressmaker to the court of Empress Eugénie and launched most of the new concepts of fashion from the late 1850s to the 1870s.

The clothing from this decade is somewhat more available than earlier styles, but it is usually bought for costume collections and museums and not normally worn. The skirts were so large, because of the hoops, that they are not functional. However, many of the mantles, capes, and accessories are still quite sturdy and show up in shops.

# OUTERWEAR

1853—Blue-and-white-striped silk dress with Juliet sleeves; gathered bodice in front and two small flounces at hem; *Mint*; $250.

1855—Very faded green cotton dress with high neck and modified square neckline; copious tucks and lace trim; *Fine*; $35.

1855—Iridescent-blue moiré silk swallowtail jacket with full-length sleeves and cording; *Excellent*; $75.

1855—Formal afternoon reception dress in royal blue with Prussian silk-velvet brocade borders; fitted bodice with pagoda sleeves and lace undersleeves and ribbon at waist; tiered crinoline skirt over hoop; courtesy Campbell House Museum, St. Louis; *Mint*; $1,000; *Not for sale*.

1855—Ecru silk-georgette dress; fabric has small polka dots; gathered and ruched full sleeves with flounces and bows; two rows of pleated flounces at bottom of skirt; scoop neck with pleated capelet covered with lace and bows; Author's Collection; *Mint*; $1,000; *Not for sale*.

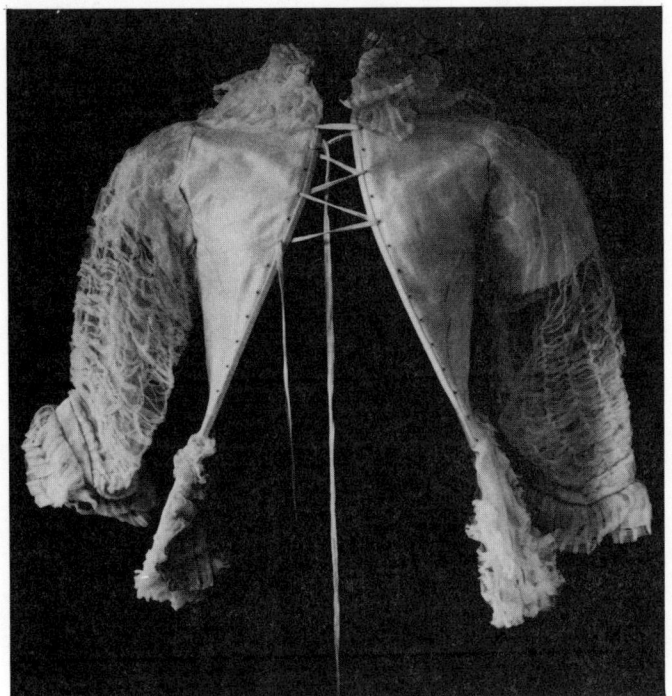

1857—Bodice with back lacing; *Poor*; $35.

1859—Black cape of net, brocade, and ribbon; *Mint*; $150.

1859—Long skirt with train in heavy white hand-loomed cotton; *Excellent*; $45.

1860—Net-type dress with multiple layers trimmed in gold and pink cording; *Fine*; $75.

1860—Three-quarter length cape in green silk with bright rose lining padded at shoulders; green fringe trim; padded lining; *Excellent*; $125.

1860—Beaded jacket with jet "rain" fringe; *Good*; $85.

1860—White silk shirt with 15″ of handmade lace and blue silk ribbon running through lace Vs; *Mint*; $100.

1860—White tissue-silk blouse; wide tucks down front and long sleeves; *Mint*; $75.

1860—Two-piece calico dress with lace inserts, leg-of-mutton sleeves, tucking on bodice; yellow with black squiggly design; courtesy FDR Drive, New York City; *Excellent*; $350.

1860—White handmade Basque-type eyelet bodice with skirt; profuse eyelet and lace inserts; flounce on skirt and sleeves; Author's Collection; *Mint;* $400; *Not for sale.*

# UNDERWEAR

1855—White nainsook bodice with lace insert in the form of a butterfly; and lace trim; *Mint*; $60.

1855—Homespun white cotton full-length nightgown with handmade eyelets and cutwork, and patchwork design on yoke; *Mint*; $100.

1855—White nainsook pullover long chemise; sleeveless with V neck and embroidered trim; *Mint*; $20.

1855—White princess-style slip with lace inserts in bodice and hem; hand-embroidered with a design of ribbon bows at bodice and hem; Author's Collection; *Mint*; $120; *Not for sale.*

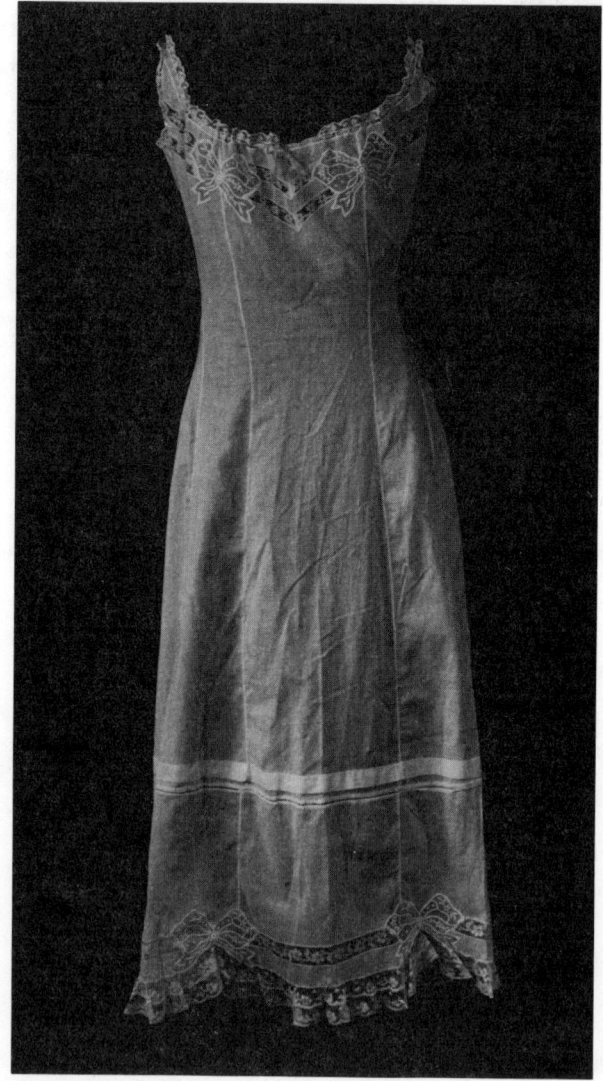

1855—One-piece white slip with intricate lace inserts, tucking appliqué; embroidered and handmade eyelets; *Mint*; $120.

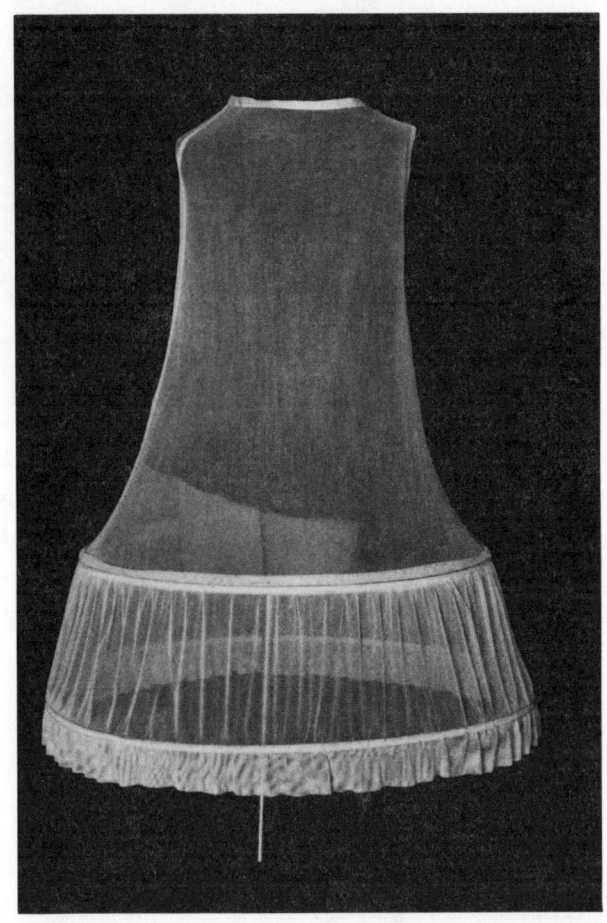

1855—Net and steel hoopskirt; courtesy Burnette Hurley Antiques, Tulsa; *Good*; $15.

1857—Flannel-lined two-tone quilted petticoat with pocket; crocheted trim; drawstring waistband; courtesy FDR Drive, New York City; *Good*; $200.

1858—Nightgown cover with drawnwork and pleating; *Good*; $175.

1859—White cotton nightgown with wide collar and intricate design of braid on collar and cuffs; *Excellent*; $115.

1860—Allover Paisley-design wool dressing gown in tones of red and gold; dropped, corded shoulder; **A**-line shape; *Good*; $125.

1860—Hand-embroidered eyelet bed jacket with inserts of handmade lace; Author's Collection; *Mint*; $150; *Not for sale*.

1860—White linen hand-loomed camisole; hand-crocheted borders and sleeves; courtesy Mount Vernon Antiques, Maine; *Excellent*; $45.

# HATS, PURSES, SHOES, AND ACCESSORIES

1855—Pink, gold, lavender, and green needlepoint purse with brass clasp and chain set with malachite beads; *Mint*; $65.

1859—White satin nightcap with lace rosebud trim; satin has small split on back; *Good*; $12.

1860—Purple silk bonnet with red roses; lining inner edge; *Excellent*; $75.

# 1861–1870

During this period dramatic changes occurred in women's attitude toward dressing. They now were able to move in their clothes instead of being held perfectly rigid. Separates appeared in the form of the first shirts or waists, skirts, jackets, and capes. The first sportswear appeared at this time, with ensembles designed for lawn tennis, croquet, and even bathing. A popular item of clothing was the braided Zouave jacket, or bolero, trimmed in ball fringe. Brilliant colors such as magenta, bright blue, and red were used for everyday, and ball gowns often combined hot pink with black. Manufactured trims were sold to match fabrics. The Greek-key design was frequently used to decorate clothing. Plaid fabrics became very popular because of Queen Victoria's residence at Balmoral in Scotland. The Swiss belt, a long sash worn with dresses, usually finished the garment. Red stockings, colored boots, and colored petticoats gained popularity, and girls in New York who wore red stockings were called "flamingos." The gored skirt provided smoothness around the hips, and skirts began to shorten in front while a small bustle continued in the back with a slight train. Sleeves became fuller and more open and showed more *engageante*.

In 1865 Dr. Mary Walker became the first American woman to wear trousers regularly. Bloomers were invented, and a great deal of time and attention was given to underwear. Skirts were pulled up by drawstrings for walking.

Because many of these pieces of clothing were more wearable in their own time they are just as wearable today. There is a lot of white Victorian underwear for sale now. In fact, in most shops, Victorian underwear usually makes up half of the stock. These petticoats, corset covers, bloomers, and so on, are usually made of wonderfully sturdy cotton, decorated with abundant lace and ribbon; they are extremely wearable. Victorian jackets, capes, and shirtwaists are being worn by many people on a regular basis as accouterments to contemporary clothing or to make a fashion statement.

# OUTERWEAR

1865—Mint-green silk capelet; lined; small pointed collar; braid trim; bone buttons; *Fine*; $15.

1865—Black jacket made entirely of ribbon and braid; fitted Basque style with pagoda sleeves; Author's Collection; *Excellent*; $400; *Not for sale.*

1865—Fillet (net) lace overblouse with Battenberg lace; *Mint*; $75.

1868—Ivory wedding dress by Hollins Pierce and Stowe, London; silk bengaline with silk fringe and crepe-de-chine trim; bishop sleeves; knotted band on skirt; courtesy Campbell House Museum, St. Louis; *Mint*; $2,500; *Not for sale.*

1869—Ecru Irish linen skirt; gored and fitted with a slight train; *Mint*; $100.

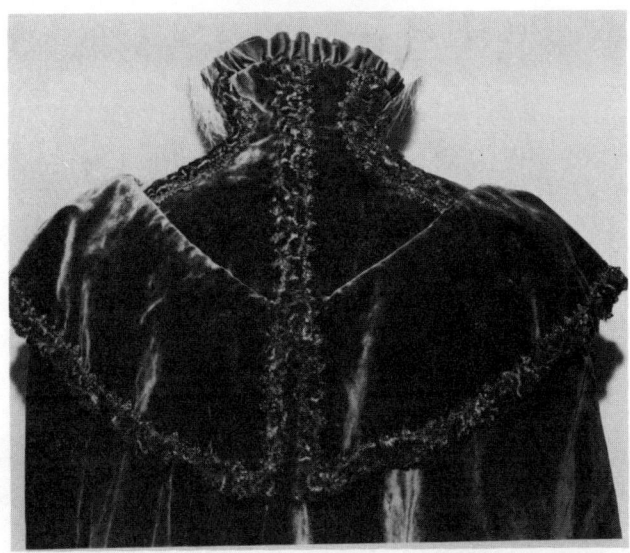

1870—Bottle-green velvet hip-length cape trimmed in jet beads and Persian lamb; upright collar with shawl effect; courtesy Sweet Emaline, Atlanta; *Mint*; $125.

1870—Black cotton dress with small pink floral-print bodice and skirt; bodice is lined in hot pink and has lace trim; skirt has four flounces at hem trimmed with lace; *Mint*; $250.

1870—White cotton bodice and skirt; lavish lace; full sleeves with cuffs; some white embroidery; *Excellent*; $175.

1870—White cotton-batiste blouse; lace and tuck insert in front and at top of sleeves, outlined in net ruffle; high, boned lace collar; snap-fasten back; *Excellent*; $65.

1870—Black cotton dress with white floral sprigs; hook-and-eye closing; small leg-of-mutton sleeves; *Excellent*; $125.

# UNDERWEAR

1861—Crocheted cotton bed jacket; *Fine*; $15.

1862—White hand-loomed cotton corset cover with hand-crocheted yoke; gathered back with tie; *Mint*; $66.

1863—Long cotton half-slip; *Good*; $30.

1865—White hand-loomed cotton petticoat with insert of hand-crocheted lace; *Mint*; $50.

1865—White batiste petticoat with 18" handmade eyelet trim at hem, also tucking; *Mint*; $85.

1864—White batiste camisole with lace inserts and handmade eyelets; *Mint*; $85.

1864—White cotton nightgown; plain; *Fine*; $16.

1865—Long white petticoat with tucks and lace inserts in 24"-long flounce; Author's Collection; *Mint*; $150; *Not for sale*.

1865—White nightgown; square neck with handmade lace and edging; *Mint*; $115.

1865—Floor-length Paisley dressing gown with train; velvet buttons; leg-of-mutton sleeves; courtesy FDR Drive, New York City; *Good*; $250.

1865—White cotton corset cover with six rows of inset drawnwork; gathered back and lace trim; *Mint*; $60.

1867—White cotton split-crotch bloomers with eyelet-lace trim; *Mint*; $35.

1870—Black silk-taffeta petticoat with drawstring waist; first ruffle approximately 6″; detailed with knife pleats and chevron tucks in triangular sections; *Good*; $30.

# HATS, PURSES, SHOES, AND ACCESSORIES

1863—Small brocade purse in red, blue, and gold with a pewter butterfly clasp with paste jewels; cane strap; *Excellent*; $65.

1865—Black woven-straw hat with silk ribbon and silk flowers; *Mint*; $75.

1870—Small black purse covered with an elaborate design in jet beads and with a ribbon handle; *Mint*; $35.

# 1871–1880

THE DISTINGUISHING feature of the 1870s costume was a jacket with tails that extended out over a large bustle. In fact, bustles in the mid-1870s were the largest ever. Brilliant colors such as pink, red, and orange continued to be popular, often with black trim. Bustles were often added as drapes *over* skirts. The bodice was normally short and tight fitting with sleeves that had oversize cuffs. Intricate patterns of tapes within the skirts could be pulled to create puffs for the extended bustle. Most necklines were square at this time. Ladies piled on as many flounces, frills, and trims as possible. Because everyone had a sewing machine, people had more clothing, and much of it survives today.

Embroidered pockets were a distinguishing feature. The short-waisted jackets of the early 1870s became longer and smoother in day dresses during the latter part of the decade. Ruching or box-pleating was a favorite decorative treatment. By the end of the decade a one-piece dress with emphasis on a "violin" shape and with a tight skirt gained favor. Lillie Langtry showed the first long fishtail train worn with this very rigid, fitted dress.

Many shops have complete outfits from this period for sale, and they are wearable for special occasions. The underwear is very visible and interesting as it conforms to the use of a bustle. Almost all of the petticoats you see are shorter and smoother in front and longer and fuller in back. Machine-made lace and lace made with chemicals began during this time and was often used in trim. Many of these garments seem very short-waisted to us, but because of the bright colors, trims, and flowers, these clothes are very feminine and fun to wear.

# OUTERWEAR

1875—Pastel flower-print netting over silk waist and skirt with bishop sleeves; waist has high neck with openwork lace inserts and ruffle over bodice; *Poor*; $100.

1872—Black and pink cotton-print bodice and skirt with some black lace trim; courtesy Laughing Cat Antiques, Houston; *Mint*; $400.

1873—Long two-piece dress in ecru silk and cotton with a faint stripe; neck and sleeves trimmed in Chantilly lace; *Good*; $95.

1875—White batiste cotton blouse with high neck; *Mint*; $90.

1875—Silk-damask dress bustle trimmed with silk-chenille fringe; worn by Mrs. Virginia Jane Campbell; *Mint*; $800; *Not for sale.*

1875—Black faille bodice with jet beads encrusted over velvet at neckline and at cuffs; *Mint*; $75.

1878—Morning coat; batiste with lace and embroidered handkerchief-type hem; courtesy Frances Altman; Atlanta; *Mint*; $125.

1878—Garden dress in figured batiste with soutache braid and open oversewn lace inserts throughout; net Juliet sleeves with extensive tucking; courtesy Frances Altman, Atlanta; *Mint*; $400.

1880—Navy-blue day dress with red and white floral calico; *Good*; $95.

1880—Tucked organza skirt with ribbon trim; ruffles at waist and hem; Frances Altman Collection; *Mint*; $175; *Not for sale*.

1880—Black silk bodice with Chantilly lace at shoulders and down front of neckline; trimmed in jet; *Excellent*; $65.

---

1880—White cotton skirt with puffing and tucking; cut eyelets and ruffle on skirt; *Mint*; $135.

---

1880—White batiste blouse with twill design; handkerchief-type neck with hand embroidery; *Mint*; $80.

---

1880—Black silk full-length cape with hood and shawl lined in black velvet; courtesy Sweet Emaline, Atlanta; *Mint*; $150.

---

1880—Black velvet wrist-length cape lined with wool; jet-bead trim; monkey fur trim on high stand-up collar and down front; *Excellent*; $125.

---

1880—Black silk elbow-length ruffled cape with jet trim; *Fair*; $75.

---

1880—White linen waist; buttoned front with wide tucks and long sleeves; eyelet design down the front and on the cuffs; courtesy Frances Altman, Atlanta; *Mint*; $135.

1880—Green and brown calico-print housedress; wool challis with green grosgrain ribbon trim; button-down front with brown glass buttons; *Good*; $125.

1880—Ivory silk-twill wedding gown; balloon sleeves ending in wide flounces of punto silk lace; large collar and neckline trimmed with lace and seed pearls; gown hangs in pleats from shoulders both front and back; not fitted except in muslin corset lining; *Excellent*; $1,000.

# UNDERWEAR

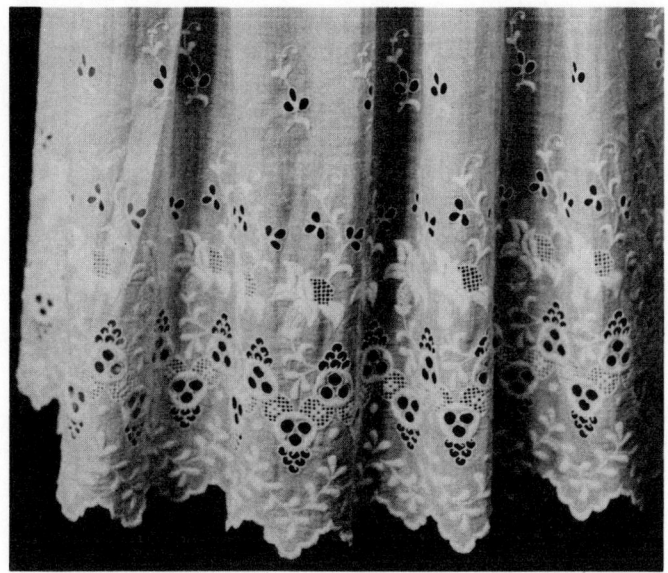

1871—White batiste petticoat with dropped waist and handmade eyelets at hem; photograph shows detail of eyelets and embroidery; *Mint*; $85.

1875—White cotton petticoat with three rows of lace inserts and tucking at hem; *Excellent*; $60.

1875—Short white cotton petticoat split for riding, with handmade eyelet; *Mint*; $24.

1875—White petticoat with tucks and overflounce with lace insert; very fancy; *Mint*; $125.

1875—Heavy white cotton slip with scallop trim; drawstring waist and handmade eyelet at hem; *Mint*; $95.

1872—Heavy white cotton camisole with four rows of drawn work; *Excellent*; $40.

1875—Organza double skirt with ruffles on hem in handkerchief design; courtesy Frances Altman, Atlanta; *Mint*; $225.

1875—Battenberg-type lace corset cover; courtesy Frances Altman, Atlanta; *Mint*; $45.

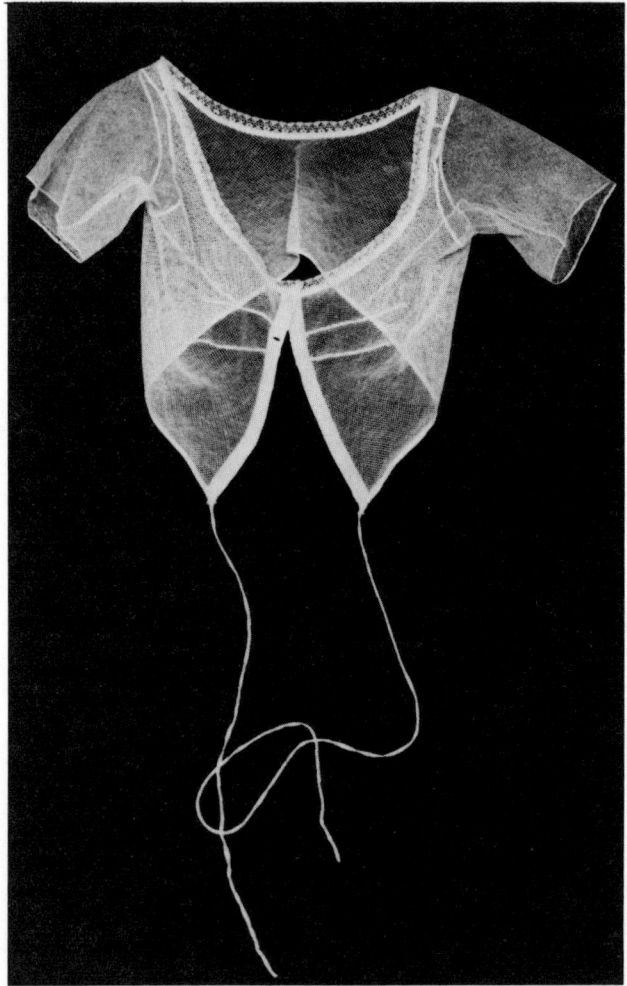

1875—Binder in white net; courtesy Burnette Hurley Antiques, Tulsa; *Perfect*; $45.

1875—White cotton nightgown with hand-crocheted yoke and crocheted insert in hem; *Mint*; $95.

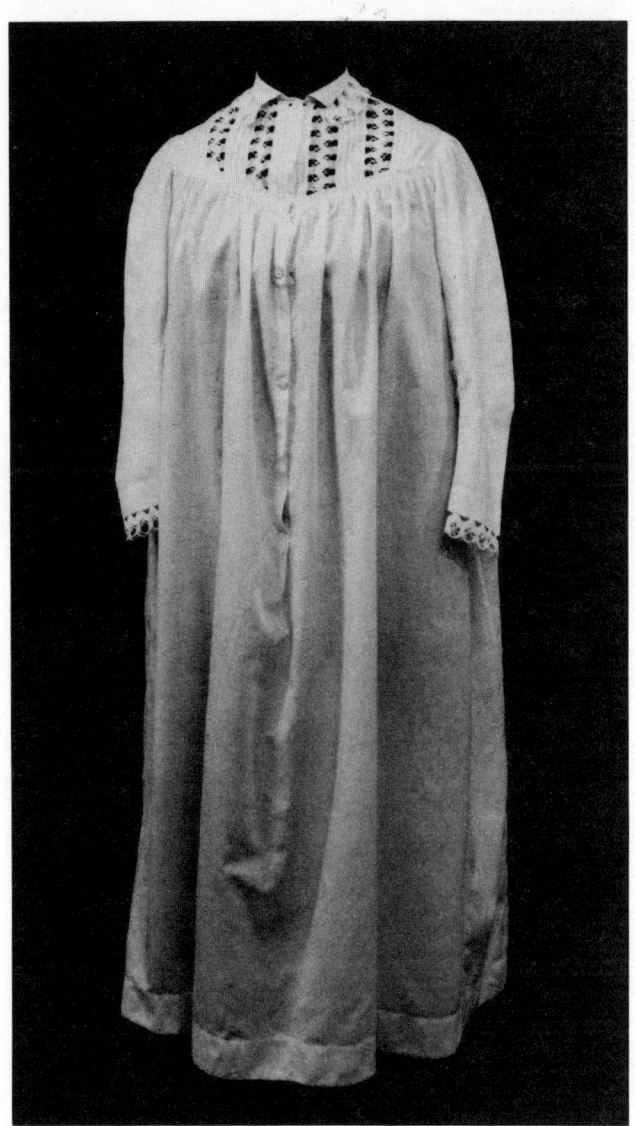

1875—White cotton nightgown with collar braid and crocheted yoke and sleeve trim; courtesy Frances Altman, Atlanta; *Mint*; $115.

1879—White handmade eyelet bed jacket with lace inserts and trim; ¾-length sleeves; *Mint*; $120.

1880—Pink and tan brocade-and-silk gown; handmade lace collar and cuffs; pink pearl buttons in tatted button holders on front bodice; *Good*; $148.

1880—White cotton sleepcoat with panels of ruching and Swiss embroidered eyelets down the front and on cuffs; *Mint*; $195.

# 1881–1890

READY-MADE CLOTHING was now regularly available in department stores. By 1880 the layering of several garments was popular. There was a division of front fullness horizontally to back fullness, which was vertical. Garments had a lot of lining and interlining, and the shoulder began to have a more natural shape. Pannier dresses, though much narrower, were popular for evening. The drape, which is similar in appearance to a pannier, became fashionable and through the decade developed from symmetrical dips into asymmetrical ones.

The single most dramatic feature was the bustle, which started small in 1881 and became like a shelf by 1885. The neckline filled in to a high stand-up collar. As the whaling industry declined, cane was used for boning. Box-pleating was a favorite trim, and the popular colors were dark wine, red, brown, midnight blue, and black. The quality of fabrics declined, and plush, matching crochet balls, and fringes were popular trims.

Two innovations were the dolman cape and the use of loose one-piece robes to be worn at home. The use of all or parts of the bodies of animals and birds as trim was stylish. Around 1890 the bustle almost faded out. Because more clothing was being made and sold at this time, more is available in shops today. However, the bustle and the elaborate draping make these clothes a little difficult to wear. They are usually not in the best shape because the fabric was chemically sized, and these chemicals tended to make fabrics such as silk and brocade deteriorate. Many collectors enjoy this period because it was so elaborate in design and trim. Many of the blouses, capes, jackets, and underwear are worn by enthusiasts and make a dramatic addition to one's wardrobe.

# OUTERWEAR

**1881**—Two-piece heavy silk-twill traveling costume of blue, green, and red plaid; braid trim and closures; *Excellent*; $600.

**1882**—French gray silk dress with bustle and fitted bodice with long sleeves, chenille trim on skirt with several layers of ruffles; lace fichu collar; marabou feather fan; *Mint*; $800.

**1882**—Brown and gold velvet-plush street dress with ribbed-silk apron drape; full-length sleeves; brown summer ermine muff and capote bonnet with feathers; Campbell House Museum, St. Louis; *Mint*; $850; *Not for sale*.

**1884**—Black velvet full-length dress with bustle back, lace jabot, lace on cuffs, buttons to waist; black velvet hat with veil; *Good*; Dress, $125; Hat, $25.

**1885**—Irish linen coat with lavish embroidery and lace inserts on front, on back, and on French cuffs; courtesy Frances Altman, Atlanta; *Mint*; $185.

1885—Basque jacket-shaped bodice ending below waist; black silk lined with white silk; front and back of bodice decorated with black passementerie cording; sleeves trimmed with heavy tassels; *Perfect*; $280.

1885—Black silk high-neck bodice and skirt with intricate embroidery; skirt has slight train and overlapping panels; Author's Collection; *Mint*; $400; *Not for sale*.

**1885**—Paisley wool jacket with chenille fringes; ¾ length with bustle; dolman half-cape sleeves; courtesy Campbell House Museum, St. Louis; *Mint*; $400; *Not for sale*.

**1885**—Off-white silk dress with velvet Spanish-style bolero; fringe on skirt; ¾-length sleeves; purple sash; *Fair*; $185.

**1888**—Rust silk skirt; silk net overskirt gathered full in back descending to train; underskirt has pleated trim at hem with beautiful off-white lace ruffle; made to be worn with coiled wire bustle or as is; rust bodice laces up front with short sleeves gathered with exaggerated puggs; gilt appliqué trim on scoop neck; *Mint*; $1,190.

**1890**—Silk-satin walking suit in iridescent rust color with leg-of-mutton sleeves on bodice; lace and metal sequin trim; *Mint*; $275.

**1890**—Two-tier white cotton dress; *Mint*; $275.

**1890**—Pink silk-chiffon and satin cape, label reads *Paquin*; ruching trim and metallic vegetable sequins; high stand-up collar; fingertip length; *Good*; $400.

**1890**—White, embroidered silk-organza bodice and skirt; skirt is two-tiered with scallops at both hems; bodice has ¾ sleeves; scalloped shawl-type collar and lace insert; Author's Collection; *Mint*; $500; *Not for sale*.

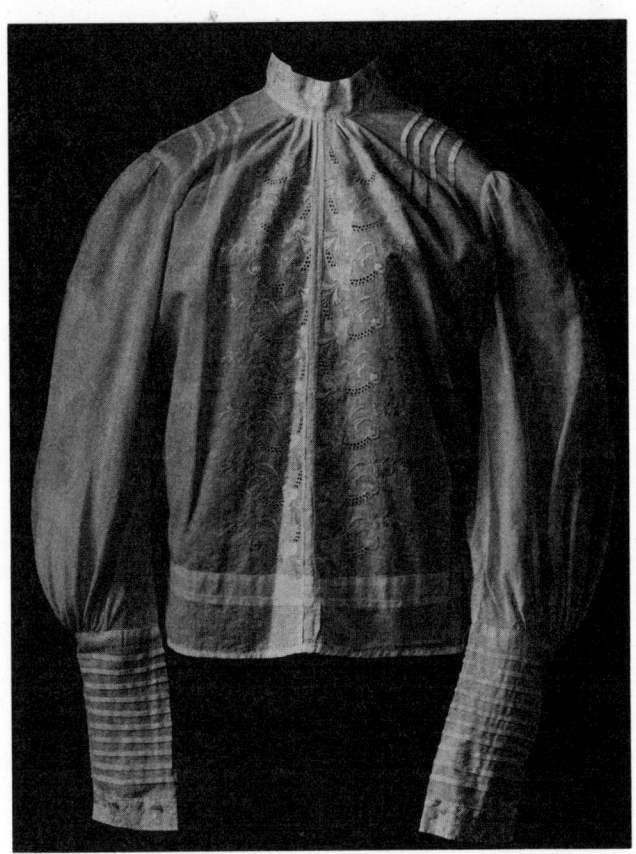

1890—White batiste blouse with heavily tucked full sleeves and high neck; Indian whitework embroidery; *Mint*; $95.

1890—Cotton-voile wedding gown with leg-of-mutton sleeves; the ensemble includes blouse, skirt, petticoat, and train; hand tucking on skirt and sleeves; *Mint*; $1,000.

1890—White batiste overblouse; open on side; *Good*; $35.

1890—Gray unborn calfskin capelet with moleskin trim and carved mother-of-pearl buttons; lined in gray silk; courtesy Laughing Cat Antiques, Houston; *Mint*; $300.

1890—Black Battenberg lace coat, midcalf length; full sleeves with deep cuffs; neckline and back draped with black macramé silk cord trimmed with jet beads and sequins; *Excellent*; $400.

1890—Battenberg lace waist with high neck and leg-of-mutton sleeves; Alice Stauber Collection; *Mint*; $125; *Not for sale.*

---

1890—Full-length white linen skirt with cord embroidery and openwork; *Mint*; $225.

---

1890—White dress with lace inserts with crocheted flowers on sleeves and down front panel; *Excellent*; $365.

---

1890—Red wool cape; quilted red silk lining trimmed all around edges (bottom, front, and neck) with peacock feathers; high stand-up collar; bead trim on strips the length of cape; label reads *Place Vendome Paris*; minor moth damage; *Good*; $225.

---

1890—Black printed-cotton housedress; ruffle at front and shoulder, braid trim, loose front; gathered belt; gathers at back of waist; *Excellent*; $85.

---

1890—Rust plush reversible cape with black crepe lining; 38″ long; some wear on Persian lamb collar; *Good*; $55.

---

1890—White cotton Gibson Girl blouse with tucked bodice and shoulders; sleeves have lace inserts; hand-embroidered floral design below tucks; *Excellent*; $55.

# UNDERWEAR

1885—White cotton camisole with handmade English whitework; *Mint*; $120.

1890—White camisole cover, embroidered with applied lace medallions; drawstring neck; *Mint*; $45.

1890—White cotton chemise; short sleeve eyelet inserts; *Mint*; $30.

1890—Ivory silk petticoat with train and ruffle around bottom; small stain; *Good*; $40.

1890—White eyelet camisole with pink satin ribbon; *Mint*; $65.

1890—Chinese export silk dressing gown, all-over pale pink embroidery; carved brass buttons; *Fair*; $80.

1890—Short white petticoat with two 4" bands of crocheted lace; *Good*; $35.

# HATS, PURSES, SHOES, AND ACCESSORIES

1885—Organza and fillet-lace privacy insert, or dickey; courtesy Frances Altman, Atlanta; *Mint*; $25.

1885—Widow's bonnet and veil; *Mint*; $65.

1885—Black lace, jet, ribbon, and egret-feather capote bonnet with pale pink flowers; *Mint*; $100.

1885—Black straw capote bonnet with jet, silk flowers, and purple velvet flowers and pompons; courtesy Campbell House Museum, St. Louis; *Mint*; $125; *Not for sale.*

1886—Cotton Arnett mitts, fingerless gloves; *Mint*; $12.

1890—Brown flocked fur hat trimmed with loops of black silk and ostrich plumes; *Perfect*; $150.

1890—Silk-taffeta drawstring bag with crocheted inserts; *Mint*; $35.

1890—Gold beaded purse with filigree brass clasp; chain strap; *Excellent*; $85.

1890—Leather hightop lace-up shoes; dressy French heel; *Mint*; $65.

1890—Mauve straw hat with flowers and feathers; *Mint*; $55.

# 1891–1900

As women became more physically active, special clothes were used for games, bicycling, and bathing. These are nothing like what we have now, but they are very relaxed compared to the clothes of the previous decade. The silhouette was wide-shouldered with wide lapels or leg-of-mutton sleeves, a wasp waist, and well-rounded at the hip. Most articles of clothing could be bought as separates, including separate belts, which developed in this period. Skirts were fairly plain, gored, and fit tightly to the foundation. This was called a bell, or umbrella, skirt. Day skirts were ankle length and evening gowns had trains. Closures, such as hooks and eyes, were designed to be invisible. The designer Worth made jet trim popular at this time. Fine materials like mohair, tussore cashmere, and linen were used. Moiré (watered silk), often in candy-striped pastels, was used for evening gowns. Black soutache braid or velvet often outlined the silhouette. Moss green was the favorite color of the time. Schiffli or machine-made embroidery began to be used predominantly in trim. Because the silhouette of this time was exaggeratedly feminine, it is very popular with people who wear antique clothes. The women were larger and more active and so the clothes fit today's woman, if she has a small waist. The waist-type blouses with high necks are very popular, as are the opera capes and jackets. Clothes from this period look less like costumes, except for the long skirts, and lend themselves to daily wear. The fabrics are nicer and softer, and the evening gowns are just as wearable at dances today as they were a hundred years ago.

# OUTERWEAR

1892—Two-piece dress; high neck, silk front; purple taffeta embroidered with white spirals; black velvet trim at elbows and hem of skirt and cuffs; tortoiseshell fan with pale pink ostrich feathers; courtesy Nifty 90's, Boise; *Excellent*; Dress, $275; Fan, $50.

1895—White net oversewn-lace blouse with high neck and elongated tight wrists; courtesy Laughing Cat Antiques, Houston; *Excellent*; $125.

1895—Beige silk-print jacket or blouse, high-neck leg-of-mutton sleeves; *Good*; $35.

1895—Top portion of two-piece outfit, French-blue print with black velvet trim, high-neck collar; *Fair*; $20.

1895—White over-embroidered net tea dress with three rows of scallops on skirt, and scallops across bodice and down sleeves; *Mint*; $150.

---

1895—White batiste high-neck blouse with full eyelet front tucks and lace trim; *Good*; $35.

---

1895—Red wool cape trimmed with black glass beads and peacock feathers; label reads *Place Vendome Paris*; *Mint*; $250.

1895—White linen hand-embroidered jacket and skirt (made by nuns in a French convent); courtesy Mount Vernon Antiques, Maine; *Mint*; $375.

---

1895—Turquoise-blue cotton high-neck tea dress with lace inserts and ruffled sleeves; *Excellent*; $225.

---

1896—Brown wool-plush jacket with leg-of-mutton sleeves and velvet insert in collar; ¾ length; *Mint*; $200.

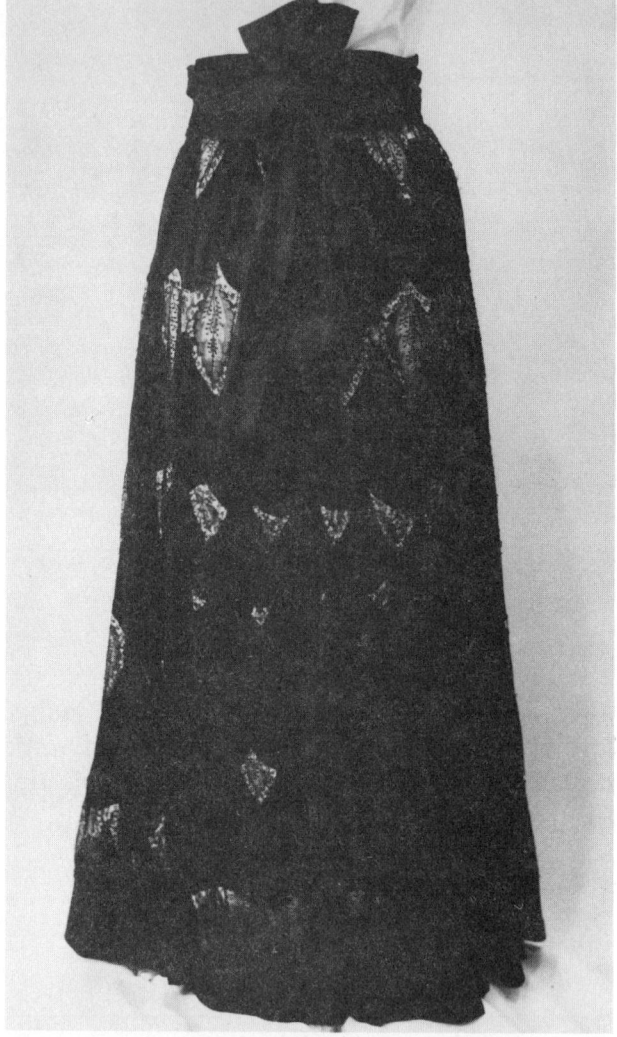

1896—Black lace skirt and top; skirt has alternating layers of lace and silk in scallops; top has dropped waist, lace inserts, and asymmetrical sleeves with full fringe; *Excellent*; $200.

1897—White linen dress with heavy embroidery; buttons down back; tatted-lace inserts; *Mint*; $450.

1898—Mourning gown of black jacquard-woven taffeta, slight train; silk widow's bonnet; full-tail cape; courtesy Campbell House Museum, St. Louis; *Mint*; $2,500; *Not for sale*.

1900—White linen schoolgirl middy blouse; long sleeves; sailor collar; *Good*; $30.

1900—White batiste garden dress with high neck, elaborate tucking, and lace inserts; narrow sleeves with a wide band over each shoulder from front to back; courtesy Frances Altman, Atlanta; *Mint*; $600.

1900—Silk-taffeta blouse; Chinese print with silk-velvet insert and sleeve trim; *Mint*; $200.

1900—Irish linen waist with high neck and shamrock embroidery; shoulders tucked and sleeves flared at end; *Mint*; $145.

1900—Ivory silk-crepe floor-length formal gown; Empire waistline with sleeves and top half made entirely of tatting; silk ribbon at neck and sleeves; *Good*; $85.

1900—Pink dotted-swiss silk dress; two-piece bodice has a square neck edged with black velvet ribbon and beaded trim; long sleeves; *Fair*; $75.

1900—Two-piece black silk dress; fabric has allover print of ivory circles; ivory lace trim on high neck and front of bodice and cuffs; *Good*; $95.

---

1900—Street-length black silk-taffeta skirt; black passementerie cording on front panel; courtesy Ages Past, Colorado Springs; *Fair*; $175. See page 45, left illustration.

---

1900—Two-piece loose-weave black silk gown with long sleeves and 4" lace ruffles at cuffs; three circles of graduated size on front of bodice and around hem of skirt in lavender and edged with tiny, black pleated ruffles; *Good*; $95.

---

1900—Edwardian batiste blouse with scoop neck and long sleeves; tucks on shoulders and sleeves; intricate Irish embroidery; opens in back; courtesy Frances Altman, Atlanta; *Mint*; $125.

---

1900—Edwardian overblouse with appliquéd flowers and embroidery; to be worn over a camisole; net sleeves; opens in back; courtesy Frances Altman, Atlanta; *Mint*; $125.

1900—White lace evening gown with lace inserts and tucks; long organza sleeves and high neck with self-bodice and self-crinoline petticoat; courtesy Frances Altman, Atlanta; *Mint*; $865.

1900—Edwardian white batiste dress yoked with ruffle; lace inserts and tucking; ruffled sleeves and hem; *Mint*; $145.

1900—Ivory silk blouse trimmed with inserted lace and satin ribbon; elaborate Battenberg lace high-neck collar; cummerbund; *Excellent*; $55.

1900—Irish crochet-lace high-neck blouse; raised rosettes and leaves; courtesy Flamingo's, Kailua-Kona, Hawaii; *Mint*; $200.

1900—Green wool full-length coat with black mouton trim, bustle, and leg-of-mutton sleeves; courtesy Early Halloween, New York City; *Good*; $300.

---

1900—Ivory Irish crochet high-neck blouse; buttons in back; slight leg-of-mutton sleeves; *Excellent*; $300.

---

1900—Typical Irish crochet, handmade blouse; *Mint*; $300.

---

1900—Pale green silk-taffeta blouse trimmed with handmade bobbin lace; courtesy Painted Lady, San Francisco; *Mint*; $400.

1900—Handmade Battenberg lace blouse; courtesy Painted Lady, San Francisco; *Mint*; $350.

1900—White linen high-neck Gibson Girl blouse; white linen jacket with soutache embroidery on wide lapels and matching white skirt with full-length tucking; straw boater with grosgrain ribbon; courtesy Campbell House Museum, St. Louis; *Mint*; $1,800; *Not for sale*.

1900—Detail of blouse of Edwardian lavender-silk day dress with embroidery and fagoting, and tucking on sleeves and skirt; courtesy Sweet Emaline, Atlanta; *Poor*, $80.

1900—Two-piece cotton outfit; Gibson Girl-type leg-of-mutton sleeves, pin tucks, and high collar; *Excellent*; $225.

1900—White batiste cutwork, front-closure blouse with tucked shoulders; *Mint*; $155.

1900—Two-piece black-and-white silk-print dress trimmed with machine lace, pin tucks; *Mint*; $225.

1900—White tissue-silk dress; full short sleeves; cummerbund; pleated ruffle on skirt; trimmed in lace; *Mint*; $200.

1900—Edwardian white lace dress with two-tier skirt; made entirely of Battenberg lace with Valenciennes lace inserts, over-embroidery, and embroidered medallions; Author's Collection; *Mint*; $1,000; *Not for sale*.

1900—Heavy cotton skirt; dust ruffle elaborately decorated with piecework lace and hand-crocheted; courtesy Ages Past, Colorado Springs; *Mint*; $200.

# UNDERWEAR

1892—White handloomed cotton camisole with crocheted yoke; *Mint*; $45.

1893—White wedding petticoat with vertical tucks and eyelet insert at waist; *Good*; $95.

1895—White eyelet open-front dressing gown with double net; collar slits for ribbons at waist and sleeves; *Mint*; $225.

1900—Edwardian white batiste underslip with fitted waist; overlap bodice with lace and embroidery; *Good*; $45.

1900—Plain white homespun cotton corset cover; *Excellent*; $25.

1900—White cotton bustle petticoat with side pocket; 72" dust ruffle of handmade eyelet 6" wide; *Excellent*; $65.

1900—Ivory satin corset; lace and ribbon trim; medium size; *Excellent*; $30.

1900—Cotton petticoat, typically French; hand-embroidered; handmade lace trim; *Mint*; $350.

1900—White cotton nightgown; leg-of-mutton sleeves; high collar trimmed with handmade eyelet lace; *Excellent*; $300.

1900—Cotton-lawn, floor-length petticoat, with longer back for bustle; 1" panels of white handmade lace, two down front, three at hem alternating with tucks; *Good*; $25.

1900—White cotton petticoat; double flounce of 10" crocheted lace; *Excellent*; $65.

1900—White batiste peignoir lined in pink cotton with embroidery and lace inserts; shawl collar; ties in front; *Mint*; $125.

1860—White cotton-voile dress patterned with large pink roses and with a square neck, and detachable net and silk sleeves; heavy ruching on bodice and sleeves; trimmed at neck, sleeves, and armholes with wide black velvet ribbon; Weinberg Collection; *Excellent*; $300; *Not for sale.*

1868—Red and black woven-satin dress with fitted bodice trimmed in jet and with scoop neck and cap sleeves; wide crinoline skirt worn over a hoop; courtesy Campbell House Museum, St. Louis; *Mint*; $1,000; *Not for sale.*

1870—Blue, white, and black silk-print bodice and skirt; the skirt has a train; the bodice has black velvet ribbon and lace with a high neck; Author's Collection; *Mint*; $500; *Not for sale.*

1879—Dress of gold and brown velvet-brocade on a satin ground with drop bustle and train; ¾-length sleeves with brown silk-ribbon trim and chenille fringe; courtesy Campbell House Museum, St. Louis; *Mint;* $1,000; *Not for sale.*

1890—Brown velvet bonnet lined in beige silk and net with ruffled edges; courtesy Campbell House Museum, St. Louis; *Mint*; $100; *Not for sale*.

1895—Plaid silk-taffeta twill traveling costume with leg-of-mutton sleeves; metallic-braid trim; courtesy Painted Lady, San Francisco; *Mint*; $400.

1895—Cream silk-faille reception dress with Watteau back and large balloon sleeves; decorated with Italian point lace and seed pearls; courtesy Painted Lady, San Francisco; *Mint*; $800.

1900—Red Chinese silk dress with lace at neck and puffed sleeves; velvet corselet encrusted with paste jewels; made in France; Author's Collection; *Mint*; $400; *Not for sale.*

1900—Pink cotton day dress with gingham blouse and embroidered cutwork jacket; straw hat with pink silk flowers; courtesy Campbell House Museum, St. Louis; *Mint*; $1,800; *Not for sale.*

1902—Deep-rose silk dress with small-scale pink geometric print; heavily beaded in multicolor pattern; lace insert at neck; sleeves with silk-braid trim; elaborate back detail with weighted panels and braid; Author's Collection; *Mint*; $600; *Not for sale.*

1905—Two-piece day dress trimmed with pin tucks and embroidered net-lace collar; courtesy Painted Lady, San Francisco; *Mint*; $225.

1910—Machine-made gold metallic-lace dress; courtesy Painted Lady, San Francisco; *Mint*; $300.

1920—Beaded flapper dress with crystal beads and green and blue sequins; skirt is cut in gored effect; rainbow feather fan; courtesy Campbell House Museum, St. Louis; *Mint*; Dress, $800; Fan, $200; *Not for sale.*

1920—Lavender panne-velvet dressing gown with ruffled shoulders and long tapered sleeves; buttons at the side with celluloid-and-diamanté buttons; gored and flared hem; courtesy Alice Stauber, St. Louis; *Mint*; $125.

1925—Black and red rayon kimono with bold multicolor print; courtesy Laughing Cat Antiques, Houston; *Mint*; $200.

1930—Cut-velvet opera coat in classic Art Deco multicolor design; silk collar and one-button closure; courtesy Alice Stauber, St. Louis; *Fair*; $150.

1900—White nightgown; crocheted yoke and hem; Author's Collection; *Excellent*; $185; *Not for sale.*

# HATS, PURSES, SHOES, AND ACCESSORIES

1895—Velvet hat beaded with jet wire; lace trim and insert; very open; courtesy Campbell House Museum, St. Louis; *Mint*; $65.

1895—Oversize plush felt hat with velvet trim and flower; *Good*; $40.

1900—Bird hat, base approximately 4″ in diameter; blue fabric covered all over in multicolor cloth flowers with small gray bird at front and a gray ostrich plume attached at back and curving to front; medium-blue netting with small attached velvet puffs all over; *Fair*; $30.

1900—Embroidered cotton and lace bonnet on wire frame encircled with large silk ribbon; *Mint*; $150.

1900—White macramé cord purse with fringe and self straps; *Good*; $25.

1900—Tan lace-up women's high-top shoes; size 7–7½; tongue missing from one shoe; *Fair*; $20.

1900—Hand-embroidered silk shawl; *Mint*; $300.

# 1901–1910

In 1902 patterns, like those from McCall's, could be purchased. The prevailing silhouette was a "pouter pigeon" front with a severe S curve, almost swaybacked. Dresses were more like jumpers over blouses, and sleeves lost all fullness and were tight again, usually ending right under the elbow. By 1905 sleeves had regained a comfortable fullness.

In 1906 the Gibson Girl personified the feminine look of the time, and most women tried to emulate her. Blouses were very fancy with high collars and hooked in back onto the waistband of the skirt. The popular colors were mostly pastel with gray or gray-and-pink combinations. A lot of beaded trim and black velvet ribbon threaded through lace was used. Cording or rows of tucks were used to help hold the softer fabrics in shape.

Fabrics tended to be filmy and thin such as voile, batiste, and net. Transparent black-and-white fabrics were used over pastel slips. This frilly feminine look is one of the most popular with enthusiasts of antique clothing. It is very available, wearable, and often in quite good condition. The sizes are reasonable, and the only problem is that the blouses are extremely short waisted in back. A three-inch peplum of soft batiste added to the back of the blouse so it can be tucked into today's skirts and pants is acceptable. Hardly any lace was handmade at the time, so do not be fooled. From this time on clothing becomes closer to our current sizes and more comfortable. Actually, anything 100 years old or older is an antique. Most people consider clothing from 1910 on to be vintage clothing, rather than antique.

# OUTERWEAR

1901—White lawn garden-party dress; high neck; lace inserts; *Mint*; $485.

1902—Edwardian silk-satin full-length dress with Valenciennes lace at neck, sleeves, and dripping down back; *Fine*; $80.

1903—Edwardian white garden dress with eyelet lace; net sleeves; high neck; *Mint*; $185.

1903—Pink lawn dress; lace inserts; high neck; *Mint*; $625.

1901—White silk evening dress with tassels and lace; courtesy Laughing Cat Antiques, Houston; *Fair*; $150.

1905—Black taffeta long-sleeve blouse with fabric-covered wooden buttons and high neck; *Excellent*; $45.

1905—Burgundy wool-blend two-piece shirtwaist with high collar; *Excellent*; $250.

1905—Two-piece white linen suit with knot buttons; sailor collar; *Mint*; $250.

1905—White linen Edwardian dress with cutwork, lace, and embroidery; *Mint*; $375.

1905—Gray and red lawn day dress with drop waist; self sash; handmade lace collar; *Excellent*; $75.

1905—Cotton-lawn dress with inserts of machine-made bobbin lace and point lace; pin-tucked bodice, sleeves, and skirt; *Mint*; $500.

1905—Edwardian ecru silk tea dress; pleated skirt with embroidery panels; top has chiffon insert at bodice and chiffon sleeves; handkerchief cuffs; courtesy Frances Altman, Atlanta; *Mint*; $185.

1905—Evening dress with hand-embroidered net lace; silk skirt front and back; metallic trim at waist; courtesy Painted Lady, San Francisco; *Mint*; $250.

1905—White Edwardian dress with heavy embroidery on bodice, sleeves, and hem; trimmed in ecru silk-satin; Author's Collection; *Mint*; $450; *Not for sale.*

1906—Red satin peasant-type skirt with black velvet stripes, braiding, and lace apron; *Mint*; $100.

1906—White cotton short-sleeve blouse; drawstring neck with eyelet trim; *Mint*; $95.

1908—White high-neck blouse with embroidered eyelet and lace inserts; courtesy Wearable Heirlooms, Cincinnati; *Mint*; $250.

1908—Black silk dress with peplum and rope braid in Empire style; skirt has six wide tucks at hem; *Good*; $175.

1908—Edwardian summer-batiste garden dress intricately trimmed with eyelet lace, Irish crochet-lace, embroidery, and lace inserts; hem trimmed in scalloped lace; courtesy Frances Altman, Atlanta; *Mint*; $325.

1910—French cotton morning dress; decorated with pin tucks and fagoting; courtesy Painted Lady, San Francisco; *Mint*; $300.

1910—White long-sleeve blouse with starburst embroidery and handmade eyelet inserts; high neck; *Mint*; $95.

1910—White linen long-sleeve jacket; white-on-white floral appliqué on front; *Good*; $45.

1910—Two-piece wool long jacket and skirt; V neck; velvet-trimmed cuffs and front; *Excellent*; $500.

1910—White embroidered day dress with extensive eyelet and embroidery on hem; courtesy Laughing Cat Antiques, Houston; *Mint*; $250.

1910—Handmade Battenberg lace jacket; courtesy Painted Lady, San Francisco; *Mint*; $400.

1910—White Irish crochet-lace jacket; fingertip length with puffed sleeves; no closure; *Mint*; $250.

1910—Lavender cotton day dress; lavender soutache braid; white lace trim; *Good*; $100.

1910—White lawn garden party-type dress; *Good*; $165.

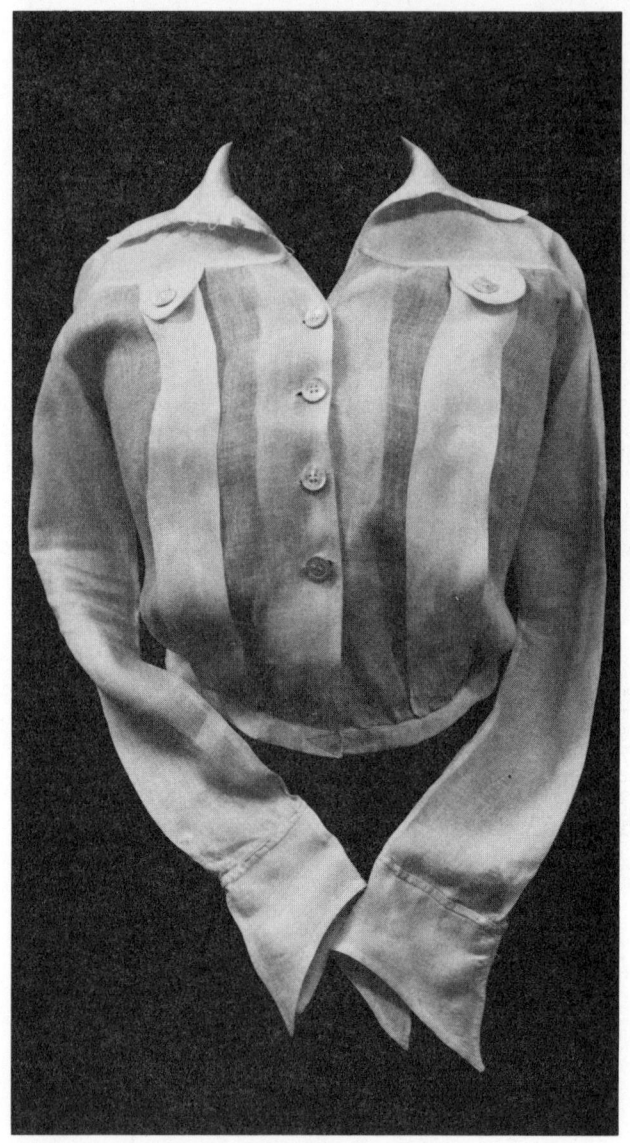

1910—Linen blouse with fitted waist and pointed cuffs; tucks and ivory buttons down front; courtesy Frances Altman, Atlanta; *Mint*; $90.

1910—White cotton-batiste confirmation dress; *Excellent*; $225.

1910—White batiste day dress with three-tier skirt; top skirt embroidered with daisies with blue centers; lace at cuffs and neck; *Mint*; $300.

1910—White oversewn-net tea dress with shawl-type collar; embroidery at scalloped hem, neckline, and sleeves; lace inserts; *Mint*; $200.

1910—Two-piece white lawn dress with white-on-white appliqués on front bodice and front skirt panel; long sleeves; *Good*; $75.

1910—Long gray cotton work dress with white stripe; high waist; buttons down front; long sleeves; black-and-white scallop trim; shell buttons; *Fair*; $25.

1910—White batiste dress with wide embroidery; *Fair*; $100.

1910—Blue silk evening dress; beige embroidered net lace; Empire waist; narrow hobble skirt; long sleeves with bead trim, V neckline; new lining; *Good*; $300.

1910—Waffle-piqué full-length jacket with linen insert; cutwork with soutache braid and French cuffs; *Mint*; $300.

1910—Very large capelet with shaped lace collar of heavy ecru lace; *Excellent*; $30.

# UNDERWEAR

1901—Crocheted-lace and cotton corset cover; *Fair*; $10.

1901—Cotton petticoat; two layers of netted lace or crocheting; *Mint*; $150.

1903—White full-length gown with pocket at hips, monogram; embroidered collar insert; *Good*; $85.

1905—White full-length princess slip; 15" lace insert at hem and lace at bodice; *Mint*; $125.

1905—White batiste full-length petticoat with drawstring waist; flared hem with 12" lace; *Mint*; $165.

1908—White petticoat/camisole combination; 25" ruffle with eyelet lace; *Mint*; $235.

1910—Black-and-white-striped cotton petticoat; trimmed with handmade eyelet; *Mint*; $125.

1910—White cotton short petticoat with lots of small tucking and some eyelet; *Excellent*; $40.

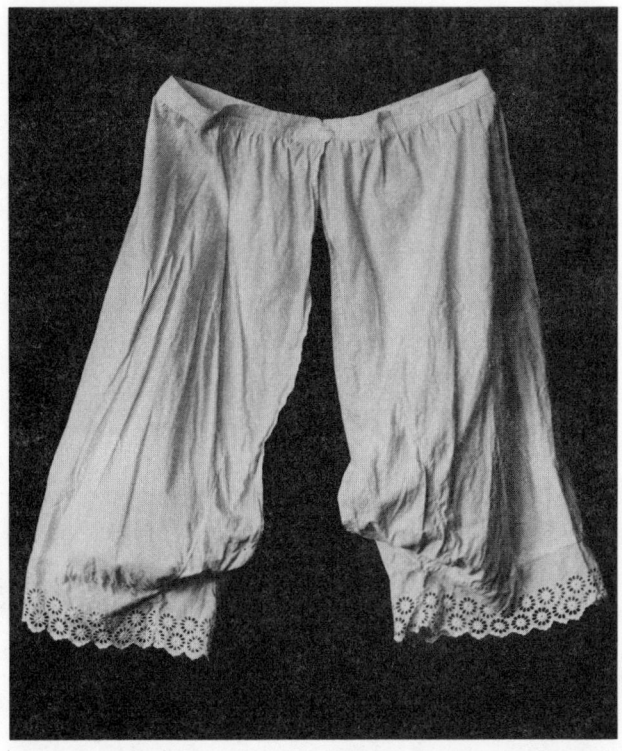

1910—White cotton split-crotch bloomers with lace trim; *Excellent*; $25.

1910—White batiste teddy with scalloped eyelet at neckline and hem, ribbons and gathers; *Mint*; $70.

1910—White cotton camisole; bobbin-lace inserts and straps; *Excellent*; $60.

1910—Hand-sewn cotton nightgown trimmed with pin tucks and tatting; *Mint*; $185.

# HATS, PURSES, SHOES, AND ACCESSORIES

1903—Edwardian detachable collar; handmade ecru lace trimmed in pink velvet and decorated with blue glass beads; *Mint*; $175.

---

1905—Belt with Art Nouveau brass clasp set with a purple glass stone; *Mint*; $45.

---

1905—Black leather lace-up shoes; size 6; shaped heel; *Excellent*; $20.

---

1905—Natural straw hat trimmed with black, brown, and peach ostrich feathers; courtesy Alice Stauber, St. Louis; *Mint*; $45.

---

1908—Multicolored velvet purse edged in gold lace with drawstring of same; *Mint*; $45.

1908—Natural leghorn straw hat with wide brim; white brocade hatband; *Mint*; $75.

1910—White parasol with embroidery on wide border; courtesy Campbell House Museum, St. Louis; *Mint*; $300; *Not for sale*.

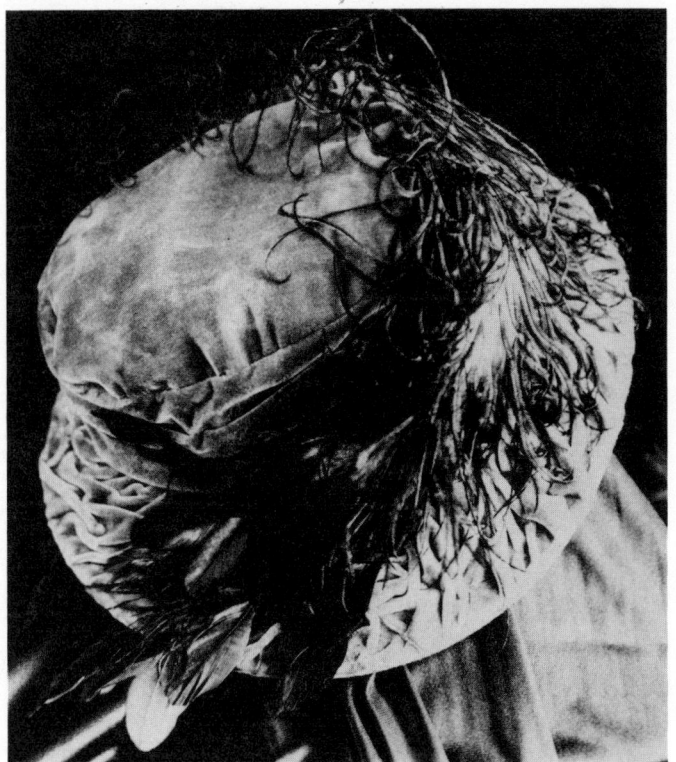

1910—Beige crushed-velvet hat with dark brown ostrich plumes and cut cock feathers; oversize crown for Gibson Girl hairstyles; *Mint*; $55.

1910—Silk and plush cloche hat with large ostrich feather; *Poor*; $15.

1910—High-top shoes with kid leather; size 5½; *Mint*; $38.

1910—Tiny red satin purse with drawstring; painted shell for body; *Excellent*; $25.

1910—German silver purse engraved "I Love You Juliet"; chain strap; *Good*; $60.

1910—Brown leather narrow lace-up shoes; courtesy Laughing Cat Antiques, Houston; *Excellent*; $25.

1910—Kid lace-up boots; two-tone black and tan; *Excellent*; $40.

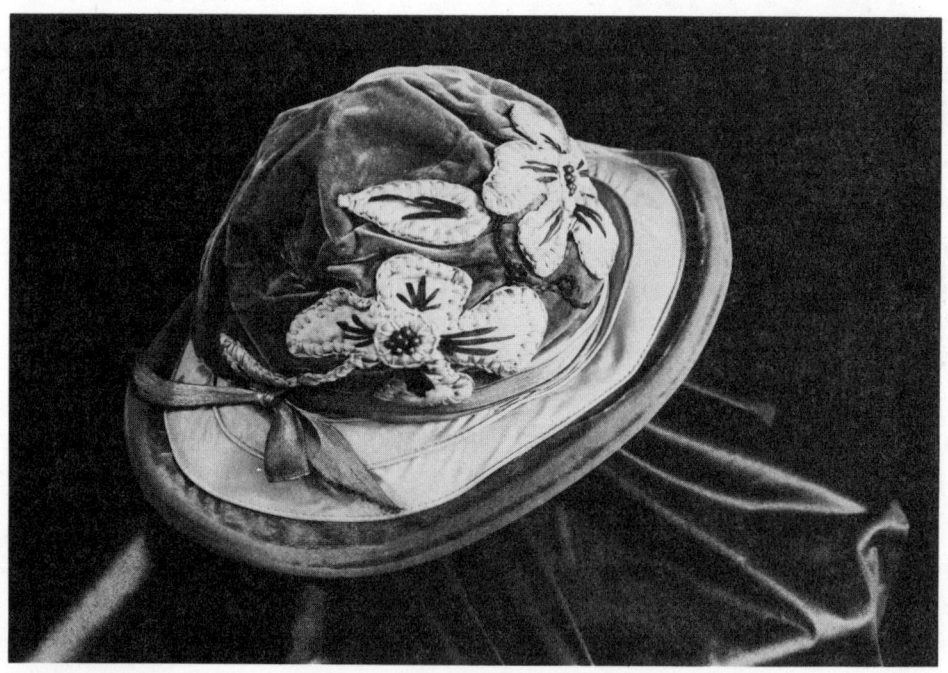

1910—Rust velvet hat with embroidered-silk appliqué flowers; courtesy Alice Stauber, St. Louis; *Fair*; $30.

# 1911–1920

By 1911 corseting had softened, and the Empire look came back into vogue. Tubelike hobble skirts and overskirts with high-waisted bodices were the mode. Fullness and detail were used high on the back. A major couturier of this time was Paul Poiret, who established this silhouette and introduced the open-neck kimono waist and set-in sleeves. He made popular the startling colors of emerald green, cerise, vermillion, and royal blue and used cerise and purple together. Two popular styles around 1913 were a tunic over a hobble skirt, which was called the "peg-top," and the "minaret," a belted tunic over a narrow skirt. After 1915 and World War I another couturier, Lanvin, brought in the full short day dress with a hem eight inches above the ground. This decade was highlighted by such major designers as Patou, Molyneaux, Bendel, and Fortuny, whose clothes are now in museums throughout the world.

Colors in the second half of the decade became more somber. Many dresses were navy blue or black and were tailored with little decoration. Fur coats and capes, which followed the lines of dresses and often had dolman sleeves, became popular. The sweater made its entrance, and the Spanish shawl returned as an important accessory. Fabrics such as foulard, satin, Charmeuse, serge, and silk crepe were used, and the famous designer Gabrielle (Coco) Chanel introduced jersey fabric to the public in 1918. It became the rage for suits. Clothes from this era are very sought after because of their high style, bright colors, and overall fantasy. The clothing will fit almost anyone as there is no strong waistline and armholes are roomy. Because many of these garments were tailor-made with fine fabrics, they are normally very available and in quite good condition. If you come across the creation of a major designer of this period such as Fortuny or Poiret, be prepared to spend thousands of dollars. A Poiret was recently sold at auction in New York for over $5,000.

# OUTERWEAR

1911—Blue-and-white-striped work dress, Empire waist; lace trim on collar and on bodice and sleeves; courtesy FDR Drive, New York City; *Good*; $115.

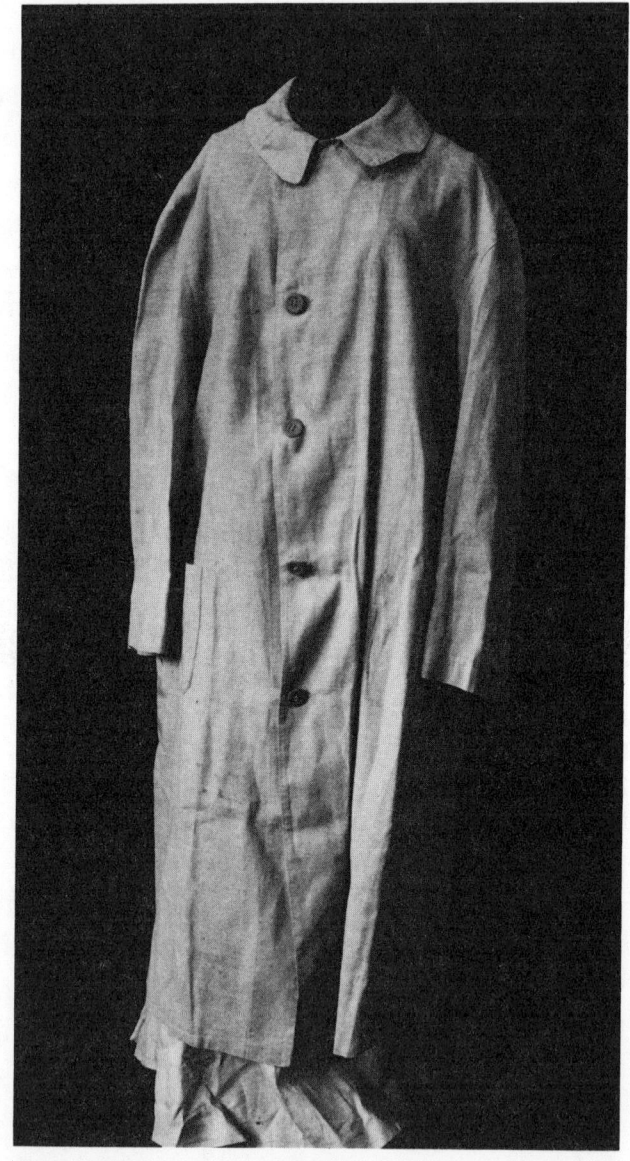

1911—Ecru linen duster for motoring; courtesy Laughing Cat Antiques, Houston; *Mint*; $75.

1911—Navy-blue silk net evening dress with long gathered sleeves; scalloped overskirt trimmed in navy satin; bodice has overblouse heavily beaded with navy bugle beads and is trimmed in satin; *Mint*; $400.

---

1912—Black silk overblouse with lace pagoda sleeves and sides; sleeves have drops and tassels; *Mint*; $125.

1912—Blue-and-white cotton-print batiste dress; lace collar; vertical-tuck front; ¾ sleeves; *Mint*; $40.

1912—White organza minaret-style dress and jacket with three-tier skirt; courtesy Laughing Cat Antiques, Houston; *Excellent*; $90.

1913—Blue-and-white gingham prairie dress with ¾ sleeves; courtesy FDR Drive, New York City; *Good*; $115.

1913—Black velvet dress lined in red silk with braid frogs; courtesy Sweet Emaline, Atlanta; *Mint*; $80.

1914—Black silk coat with scarf neckline; batwing sleeves shirred at shoulder; lined in black-and-white polka dot silk; black velvet hat with feather; black velvet purse with gold clasp; courtesy Nifty 90's, Boise; *Excellent*; Coat, $215; Hat, $50; Purse, $50.

1914—Brocade evening coat shot with silver thread; trimmed with fur; courtesy Nifty 90's, Boise; *Excellent*; $250.

1915—Pale green net evening dress with slip; extremely wide skirt; *Excellent*; $125.

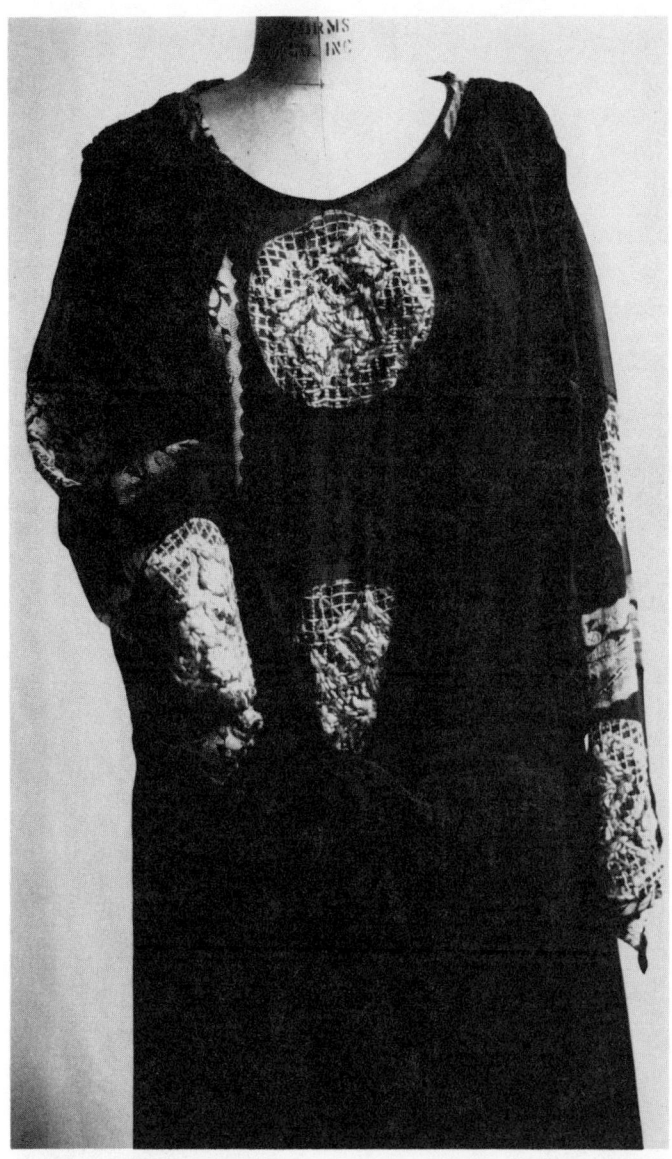

1915—Black silk-chiffon dress with pleated overdress; both are trimmed with intricate embroidery over brocade; courtesy FDR Drive, New York City; *Excellent*; $225.

1915—White oversewn net tea dress and jacket; *Mint*; $175.

1915—Black-and-white-striped silk evening dress; long sleeves trimmed with jet buttons front and back to look like a man's vest; *Good*; $300.

1915—Black wool hobble skirt with pocket; gathered in back; *Mint*; $35.

1915—Teal-blue velour suit with hobble skirt; embroidery on jacket; tucking top to bottom on underskirt-overskirt; *Good*; $155.

1915—Cotton blouse, pin-tucked bodice trimmed with bobbin lace and embroidery; totally hand-sewn; made in France; *Mint*; $200.

1915—Bloomer-skirted swimsuit, navy-blue wool blend; sailor style; *Excellent*; $175.

1915—Batiste day dress with square yoke; short sleeves; scalloped hem; heavily embroidered with garlands of flowers; *Mint*; $55.

1915—Tiered white cotton party dress; machine-made embroidery; inserted lace; crocheted buttons; *Good*; $125.

1915—Black panne-velvet mid-length opera coat; white silk lining; cape-type collar; full sleeves with lots of gathers at cuffline; buttons at side under collar; *Excellent*; $60.

1915—Cream hopsack day dress with Cluny lace and embroidered cutwork on bodice and skirt; trimmed on bodice, skirt, and back peplum with self-covered embroidered buttons; *Excellent*; $185.

1915—Two-piece linen ¾-length walking suit; hand-embroidered; celluloid buttons; *Mint*; $350.

1915—Wine Lurex dress shot with silver thread; long sleeves; full-length with asymmetrical shape; *Excellent*; $75.

1915—White linen walking suit; openwork braid sections in jacket and skirt; *Excellent*; $135.

1918—Peach silk-velvet opera coat with applied mohair-lace yoke and sleeves; gathered with buttons at hip; blue silk lining; courtesy Sweet Emaline, Atlanta; *Excellent*; $200.

1918—Silk-chiffon and machine-made lace dress; metallic floral embroidery; courtesy Painted Lady, San Francisco; *Mint*; $250.

1918—White batiste sleeveless tea dress with dropped waist; highly embroidered at hip and down front; *Mint*; $125.

1919—Navy silk-chiffon dress with orange, fuchsia, and aqua baguettes; floor-length with double-ruffle sleeves; *Excellent*; $200.

1919—White net dress with over-embroidery; sleeveless; low waisted; square neck; *Good*; $95.

1920—Two-piece hot-pink crepe dress with pleats in skirt and geometric detail at tie neck; same detail on long sleeves and ties at sleeves; *Good*; $80.

1920—Black-and-white, cotton-gingham calf-length day dress; very long wraparound ties extending out of front collar; *Excellent*; $25.

1920—Scoop-neck silk dress with a flocked scrollwork design worked into neutral background; uneven hemline dips in back; *Good*; $45.

1920—Cotton tea dress; heavy hand embroidery on bottom portion; *Mint*; $42.

1920—Full-length white ermine fur coat with hot pink velvet lining; full white fox collar; dolman sleeves; *Good*; $85.

1920—Floral-printed net evening dress in rose and pink with triple-tier skirt; pink satin underslip; *Mint*; $85.

1920—Ermine and fox coat; courtesy Alice Stauber, St. Louis; *Mint*; $325.

1920—Beaded flapper dress; black chiffon with sequins in flower pattern; *Mint*; $200.

1920—Champagne silk-satin flapper dress with tiers of loosely gathered ruffles from waist down; V neck and deep cut back of sheet silk; row of ribbon flowers down front; *Fair*; $65.

1920—Beaded black sheath with crepe chiffon; slip; *Excellent*; $125.

1920—Heavy beaded dress, black with black and white beads; made in France; *Mint*; $95.

1920—Dress made from Asyût (Asyût is a hand-embroidered fabric named after the town of Asyût in Egypt); ground is machine-made cotton net; handmade decoration is in copper with silver wash; courtesy Painted Lady, San Francisco; *Mint*; $200.

1920—White lawn dress, hand-embroidered and with handmade fillet inserts; *Mint*; $350.

1920—White tea dress with flower and lace inserts; dropped waist; asymmetrical hem; *Mint*; $150.

1920—Forest-green chiffon flapper dress; sleeveless with scoop neck; gathered and layered skirt; *Good*; $65.

1920—Molyneaux dress with his label; sleeveless white panne velvet; heavy pearl and rhinestone beading in iris motif at waist and hem (see detail photograph); Author's Collection; *Mint*; $1,000; *Not for sale*.

1920—Flesh-tone rayon-crepe georgette flapper dress; alternate rows of tucks and fagoting from neck to hem in front; plain back; long narrow sleeves with fagoting; *Good*; $40.

1920—Flesh-tone lace party dress, bias cut, sheer; low V front and back; sleeveless with matching short jacket with exaggerated cap sleeves; *Good*; $25.

1920—White batiste day dress with dainty embroidery; dropped waist; *Mint*; $185.

1920—White net peasant blouse with cap sleeves and drawstring; *Mint*; $45.

1920—White linen tea dress with embroidery; low belted waist; *Mint*; $175.

1920—Peach silk sleeveless blouse with French seams; embroidered all over with "The Rose"; *Excellent*; $65.

# UNDERWEAR

1911—Pink silk full petti-pants; *Mint*; $25.

1911—Silk teddy with lace trim; *Mint*; $28.

1912—Cotton corset cover with crocheted or netted lace; *Mint*; $30.

1915—Chemise trimmed with handmade French lace; *Mint*; $145.

1915—Cotton petticoat with inserts of handmade fillet lace; *Mint*; $400.

1917—Cotton flannel gray-and-lavender print dressing sacque; shirring on shoulders; belted; *Mint*; $35.

1918—White cotton-jersey sleeveless slip with scoop neck; *Excellent*; $30.

1920—Trousseau gown in red with blue rosettes; hand-crocheted yoke extending to waist; silk ribbon at waist with crocheted cherry design; *Mint*; $180.

1920—Simple long white gown; some tucks at shoulders with slight embroidery; *Excellent*; $50.

1920—Rayon kimono, turquoise with red, gold, pink, and navy floral sleeves banded in gold-cord rope-type belt; *Excellent*; $20.

1920—Ecru satin wide-leg panties with scallop and net trim; *Mint*; $10.

1920—Champagne silk nightgown with re-embroidered lace appliquéd all over; *Mint*; $75.

1920—White low-hipped slip with eyelet trim; *Mint*; $65.

# HATS, PURSES, SHOES, AND ACCESSORIES

1911—Black velvet-plush hat trimmed in silver ribbon; courtesy Laughing Cat Antiques, Houston; *Mint*; $75.

1915—Black velvet box-shape hat with feather; *Excellent*; $50.

1915—White straw hat; large brim upturned on sides; white ostrich feathers encircle brim; *Excellent*; $48.

1915—Navy and white pleated ribbon boater with veil; *Good*; $65.

1918—Green velvet hat with large rosettes; courtesy FDR Drive, New York City; *Mint*; $135.

1918—Aubergine straw hat with floral trim of silk velvet and silk wheat; *Mint*; $135.

1920—Wing-shaped beige silk-brocade hat; gold lace trim, silk flowers at front; courtesy Nifty 90's, Boise; *Excellent*; $45.

1920—Pink felt hat with pink flowers; *Mint*; $27.

1920—Blue felt hat; ostrich feathers cover crown and encircle brim; *Excellent*; $50.

1920—Cloche-style hat made entirely of woven metallic golden threads with gold sequin trim; and small rolled brim in front; *Excellent*; $35.

# 1921–1930

THE WAIST TOTALLY disappeared during this decade. The center of interest was at the hemline with the uneven handkerchief look or overtunic going from eight inches above the ground to touching the knee in 1925. This was the shortest that skirts had ever been and was the heyday of the "flapper." For the first time in fashion history the foundation garment was worn next to the body. At last the body was free of corsets. Beltlines stayed at the hip, and floating panels, scarfs, and gathered sections adorned skirts. New necklines included the bateau and the cowl.

The mainstay of any wardrobe was the "little black dress" in jersey, crepe, or crepe-georgette. Synthetic fabrics such as artificial silk and silk-velvet were used and had great draping qualities. Sports clothes in tweeds, wool jersey, and angora fabrics were quite popular. Pajamas were introduced and also pants for sportswear. Playsuits such as children's rompers were worn at home or at the beach, and awning-striped skirts were common in the summer.

Because clothes became much more specialized, more clothes of this period are available to the buyer. They fit well and certainly have more style and custom tailoring than we see in contemporary clothes. Most important, these clothes look similar to what we wear now and do not seem like "costumes." A lovely chiffon evening dress from 1928 would look appropriate anywhere one would wear a 1983 evening dress, yet it would cost less, be better constructed, and be unique.

Clothing from this decade is highly collected and worn daily. After all, the "early Katharine Hepburn"—oxfords, ankle socks, and angora sweater—was the first preppy look.

# OUTERWEAR

1921—Black beaded shift with new lace bodice (needs repair); beaded design on skirt; jet beads over shoulder; thin beaded straps; *Fair*; $50.

1921—Yellow silk-georgette drop-waist dress; hand-beaded flowers (blue, orange, and green beads) on bodice and around hemline; orange silk slip; sleeveless; round neckline; *Excellent*; $85.

1921—Hot pink silk-chiffon dress lined with tissue silk; loosely draped capelike collar on sleeves; V neckline; flowing panels adorn the low-waisted torso; full skirt with uneven handkerchief-style hem; rhinestone trimmings; *Excellent*; $80.

1921—Black silk-chiffon dress embroidered with crystal bugle beads in an Art Deco pattern; courtesy FDR Drive, New York City; *Mint*; $425.

1921—Silver lace shift in an allover pattern; deep mulberry velvet hem and cap sleeves with silk flowers; courtesy Nifty 90's, Boise; *Excellent*; $65.

1921—Beige woolen coat trimmed in epaulet fashion with bias bands; designed by Mignapouf; *Mint*; $160.

1922—Periwinkle blue silk-chiffon evening gown cut on the bias with gores at hem; trimmed at neckline with Chantilly lace; *Mint*; $300.

1922—Cream cut-velvet full-length coat; aqua silk-chiffon lining; kimono sleeves; drop hips; courtesy Early Halloween, New York City; *Good*; $200.

1922—Black satin blouse and skirt; straight skirt with tucked overblouse with V neck and gold insert; *Mint*; $125.

1922—Knee-length royal-blue silk dress with gold lamé floral pattern overdress; drop waist; bare shoulders; square neck; *Excellent*; $65.

1922—Ecru silk middy blouse with placket front; *Excellent*; $30.

1922—Flapper dress in straight silhouette totally covered with iridescent blue sequins in a chevron design; courtesy Laughing Cat Antiques, Houston; *Excellent*; $300.

**97**

1923—Yellow, blue, and red silk-chiffon short flapper dress; ruffles and wide yellow band on hip; *Mint*; $110.

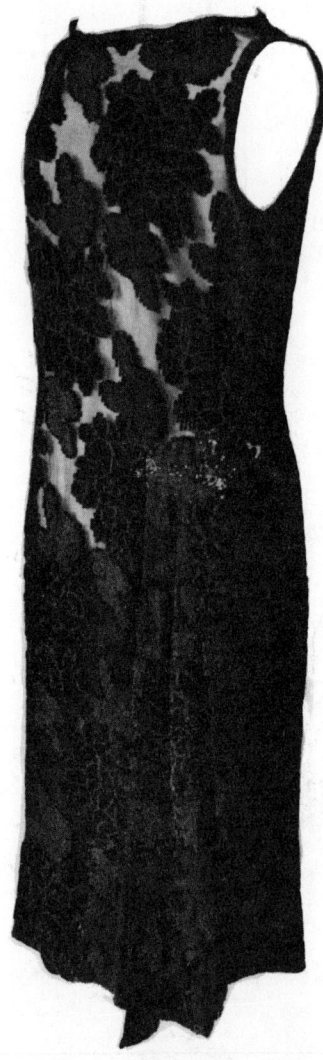

1923—Black cut-velvet sleeveless dress; side drape decorated with jet beads; *Mint*; $200.

1923—Pink-and-rose print silk-chiffon evening dress with matching jacket; long ties and gored skirt; trumpet sleeves; *Mint*; $225.

1923—Dark blue serge bolero trimmed with frogs; blue, red, and white skirt; designed by Lanvin; *Mint*; $180.

1924—Black satin dress; cowl-collar drop-waist jacket with tie; green skirt with embroidered band; courtesy Early Halloween, New York City; *Mint*; $300.

98

1925—Black wool bathing costume; courtesy Naver Collection, Houston; *Fair*; $45; *Not for sale*.

1925—Chanel black beaded tunic-style dress with small sleeves; beading done in overall geometric pattern; some discoloration of silk; large beaded tassels fall from drop waist; *Good*; $600.

1925—Long sheath dress completely covered in iridescent sequins in green, blue, and white leaf design; *Excellent*; $600.

1925—Beaded dress; black and white glass beads on silk-georgette; hip sash trimmed with black silk-velvet; *Mint*; $600.

1925—Tango-orange and lamé sleeveless dress; drop waist; *Excellent*; $200.

1925—Purple silk-panne velvet opera suit; pale chiffon blouse and jacket; full-length skirt; *Excellent*; $175.

1925—Silk-screen lamé opera coat; blue-green with fuchsia sleeves; collar trimmed with white fox; *Excellent*; $300.

1925—Opera coat; silk-screen and metallic fabric in fuchsia and blue; hood and cuffs trimmed in white fur; *Excellent*; $300.

1925—Hand-embroidered French net-lace dress; *Mint*; $700.

1925—Hand-embroidered net dress; trimmed with handmade lace; *Mint*; $400.

1925—Jeanne Lanvin silver lace dress; sleeveless; paste trim at drop waist; *Excellent*; $600.

1925—Evening dress; gold lamé top; gold lace skirt over pale green silk chiffon; decorated with metallic and silk flowers; *Mint*; $600.

1925—Beaded dress; skirt and overblouse completely covered with silver bugle beads; *Mint*; $800.

1926—Brown sheer silk, flapper-style dress with tucks arranged in geometric steps at waist; bodice and sleeves of ecru lace and embroidery; *Excellent*; $85.

1927—Black silk-crepe-satin day dress; slight gather at shoulder yoke; straight silhouette with smockinglike gather at drop hipline on each side; dark turquoise sailor-type "dickey" insert with six double rows of black glass buttons and attached long tie collar; dark turquoise trim on long sleeves; *Fair*; $38.

1927—Pink georgette dress with sequins and bead trim; matching coat with 15" fringe; feather boa; *Good*; Dress, $175; Boa, $50.

1928—Black chiffon dress in straight silhouette with lace inserts and draped collar; *Mint*; $175.

1928—Heavily beaded black silk-chiffon dress; drop waist; sleeveless; *Excellent*; $150.

1929—Black net bolero with gold sequin design; short sleeves; *Excellent*; $125.

1930—Blue-and-white chiffon blouse with puffed sleeves and camisole; *Mint*; $55.

1930—Long white dotted-swiss dress; voile matching jacket; white-and-red chiffon flower in center; *Excellent*; $135.

1930—Blue-and-white print rayon day dress; long sleeves; self belt; pearl button; *Mint*; $75.

1930—Multicolor silk-chiffon dress with bias-cut sleeves and peplum ruffles; courtesy FDR Drive, New York City; *Excellent*; $185.

1930—Dark brown rayon-velvet evening dress; short sash ties in back; draped, weighted neckline; short sleeves; *Mint*; $100.

1930—Deep purple-violet dress with leg-of-mutton short sleeves, gathered V neck, and bias-cut skirt, all of taffeta; slit in back to waist; *Mint*; $50.

1930—White chiffon evening dress with scoop neck and butterfly sleeves encrusted with beads, diamantés, and sequins; courtesy Alice Stauber, St. Louis; *Good*; $125.

1930—Two-piece pink silk day dress with matching jacket; pleated skirt; *Mint*; $85.

1930—Black crepe-backed satin bias-cut gown; cap sleeves; covered buttons; 6' double hip sashes to be tied at either side or in front; *Mint*; $95.

1930—Peach silk sleeveless evening dress cut on the bias; organza ruffle at neck; split to waist in back; *Mint*; $90.

1930—Pale peach net-and-silk sleeveless evening dress; rounded V front and back neckline; heart-shape silk underlining; 3" U-shape pieces of net sewn onto bodice but left hanging loose over skirt; lavender velvet ribbons tied into corsage effect pinned at shoulder; *Fair*; $35.

1930—Platinum crepe-backed satin bias-cut gown; covered buttons; dramatic dolman sleeves; slit to small of back; *Excellent*; $88.

1930—White brocade evening coat with gold thread trimmed at collar and cuffs with white ermine; *Excellent*; $250.

1930—Chinese top; short kimono-type sleeves; boat neckline with slit in front; silk brocade in turquoise, gold, gray, and orange with metallic thread woven in; fits loosely at shoulders and tapers at waist; fabric belt; *Good*; $40.

1930—Black lace evening dress with silk underslip; full-length V front; deep V back; cap sleeves; *Excellent*; $40.

1930—White satin evening dress; bias cut with lace dolman-sleeve jacket; self belt; *Mint*; $75.

1930—Pale pink silk-satin floor-length sleeveless evening gown; low scoop neckline; deep squared back; fitted to cling with bias-cut inserts; bias-cut flounce from hip to knee; *Excellent*; $40.

1930—Black wool-crepe dress lined in silk, cow fur trim at neck; ornament in silver and gold; *Mint*; $50.

1930—Pale blue chiffon evening dress with oversize puffy sleeves; lace inserts down front of dress; very gathered over bosom; *Fine*; $75.

1930—Pale blue net-over-net evening gown with sequin pattern; *Poor*; $45.

1930—Royal blue silk-velvet evening gown; flowing classic style; *Excellent*; $60.

1930—Floral print off-the-shoulder silk dress with blue ribbon straps; self belt; *Mint*; $65.

1930—Black silk-velvet evening coat trimmed with ermine; *Excellent*; $125.

1930—Black panne-velvet opera coat lined in white silk; dolman sleeves and shawl collar; *Mint*; $150.

1930—Moss green silk-velvet cape; has hood and satin lining; formal length; *Excellent*; $65.

# UNDERWEAR

1925—Pink satin dressing gown; beige lace insert and trim; bias cut; zipped front; *Mint*; $38.

1928—Pink silk short chemise-style slip with lace; *Mint*; $20.

1928—Cotton housecoat in bamboo print with kimono sleeve trimmed in lace; *Good*; $35.

1928—Black silk-chiffon teddy with floral embroidery on top; scalloped bottom and waist ribbon; *Mint*; $65.

1930—Peach silk-satin nightgown with matching lace trim on bodice and on shoulders; *Mint*; $18.

1930—Pale yellow nightgown with cap sleeves; lace trim and shirring in front; *Good*; $12.

1930—White rayon gown and robe combination with pastel zinnia floral design; full-length robe has banded waist that ties in front; short sleeves; sleeveless gown is smocked at shoulders; *Excellent*; $30.

1930—Peach silk teddy; cutout sides and bra-type snapping in back; lace trim on bodice and legs; *Mint*; $30.

1930—Black silk-satin floor-length dressing gown; reversible to baby blue; scalloping on collar, down front, and at hemline; *Excellent*; $40.

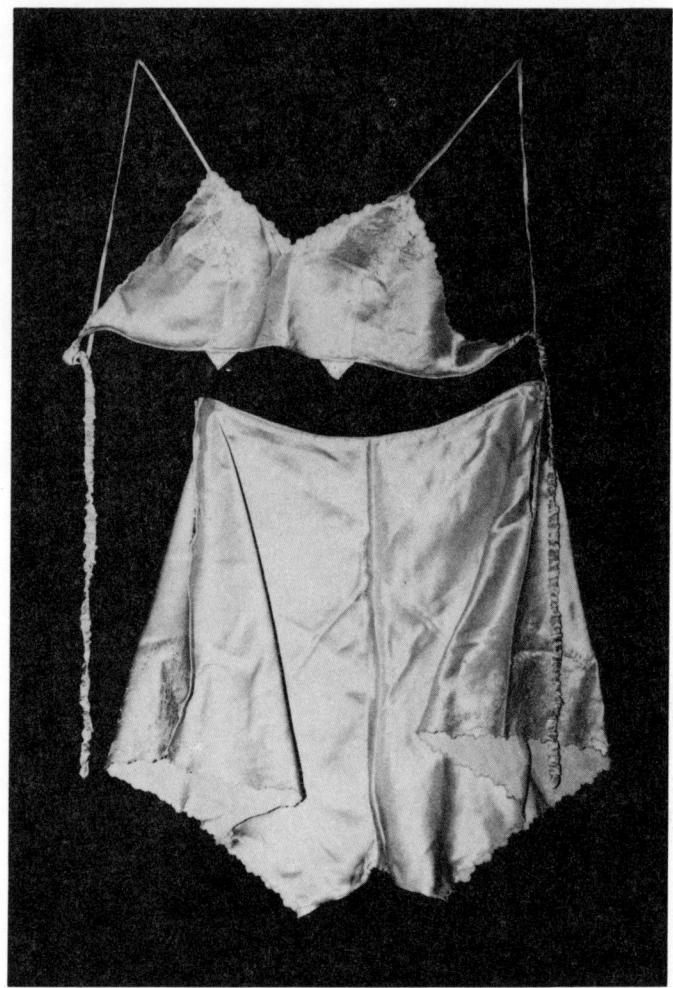

1930—Peach silk panties and matching bra handmade in China; scalloped edges with embroidery and drawn work; courtesy Sweet Emaline, Atlanta; *Mint*; $55.

1930—Pink silk-satin robe and gown with machine-made lace; bias cut; *Mint*; $100.

1930—Cream rayon sleeveless nightgown with U neckline and lace shawl-type collar; *Mint*; $22.

# HATS, PURSES, SHOES, AND ACCESSORIES

1921—Black straw hat with machine-made lace trim; rhinestone arrow pin; courtesy FDR Drive, New York City; *Excellent*; $54.

1921—Beaded bag in crystal blue and yellow flower design with drawstring strap; *Excellent*; $60.

1921—Black leather shoes with six straps encrusted with marcasite beads; medium heel; courtesy Laughing Cat Antiques, Houston; *Mint*; $50.

1921—Tiara to go with a flapper dress; beaded and encrusted with paste jewels; very rare; *Good*; $100.

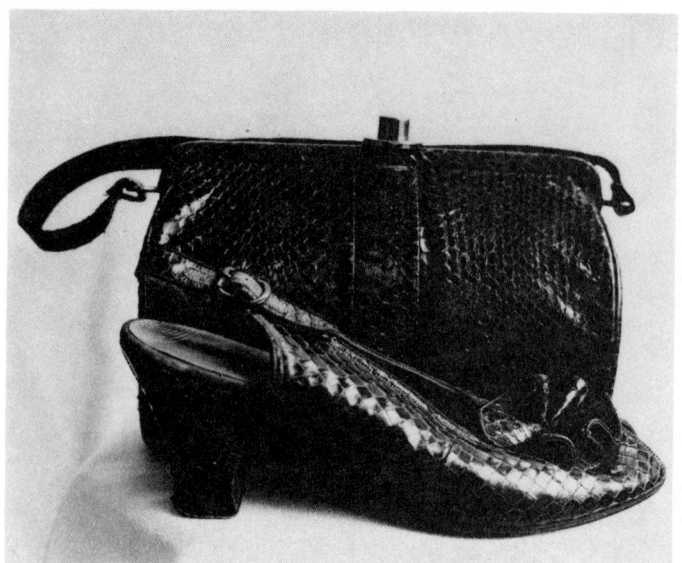

1925—Alligator bag with two compartments with matching shoes; courtesy Early Halloween, New York City; *Excellent*; Bag, $42; Shoes, $45.

1925—Enamel mesh evening bag by Whiting and Davis; *Excellent*; $50.

1925—Black leather shoes with three straps encrusted with heart-shaped marcasite beads; *Mint*; $50.

1925—Cut-silk-velvet shawl fringed with silk; *Excellent*; $250.

1925—Egyptian shawl; Asyût cotton-mesh fabric decorated with metal in geometric design; *Excellent*; $350.

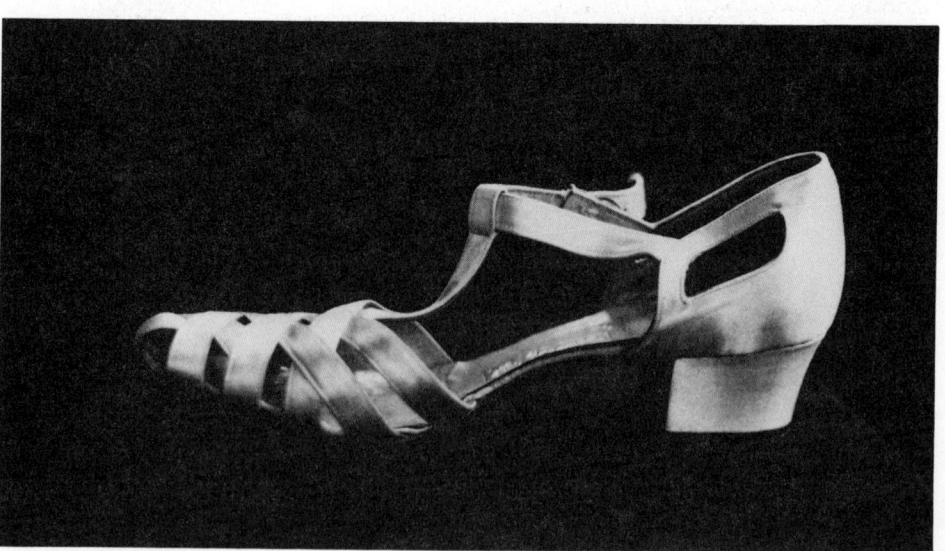

1925—White satin T-strap shoes with basket-weave effect; low heel; courtesy Early Halloween, New York City; *Good*; $45.

1926—Orange silk shawl with deep fringe and brilliant multicolor embroidery; courtesy Nifty 90's, Boise; *Excellent*; $135.

1927—Black and cream celluloid bag with rhinestones; courtesy Early Halloween, New York City; *Mint*; $95.

1927—Natural and dark gray basketweave straw hat; *Excellent*; $100.

1930—Silk shawl with silk-embroidered flowers; *Mint*; $125.

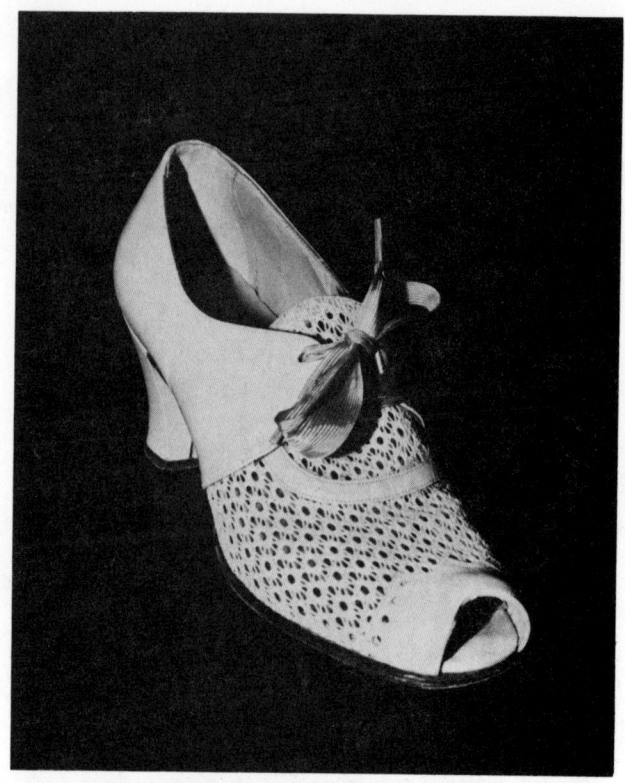

1930—Bone leather daytime walking shoes with lattice weave; open toe; courtesy Alice Stauber, St. Louis; *Mint*; $10.

1930—Elegant black lace shawl worn by Gertrude Lawrence at the Cape Playhouse, Dennis, Massachusetts; *Excellent*; $65.

1930—Black sequin skullcap-shaped cocktail hat with egret plume; *Mint*; $35.

1930—Small aqua-blue velvet drawstring evening bag; rhinestones and brass tips on drawstring; *Excellent*; $12.

1930—Burgundy satin slippers; rhinestone accessories; *Excellent*; $12.

## 1931–1940

By this time clothes had become so highly specialized that there were clothes for every occasion, and people had many more of them. The waist came back, and Mae West in an 1890s costume as Diamond Lil inspired a resurgence of the fitted-body look. The all-in-one brassiere and girdle helped to create this form. Day-dress hems were about eight to ten inches off the ground and evening dresses were full length. The tailored, mannish-looking pants ensembles were standard for sports. The halter (or bare midriff) and one-piece short bathing suits were popular at resorts and beaches. Skirts, blouses, sweaters, and jackets could be combined to form many different looks. The most dramatic silhouette was the padded, wide-shouldered suit with a straight or gored skirt. Garnet red, eggplant purple, chartreuse, vivid pink, and lime green were favorite colors. Dresses with jackets for both day and evening were fashionable. Some famous designers of this prewar era were Balenciaga, Schiaparelli, Rochas, Mainbocher, and Vionnet.

Many current dresses, suits, and separates have been exactly copied from this period. Many of the original garments have survived because they are not that old and because so many were made. They are still very reasonable in price, often costing less than contemporary clothes. During this decade sizes became standard and correspond to what we wear today. The evening clothes were elegant; the daytime clothes smart; and the sports clothes were wonderfully fashionable.

# OUTERWEAR

1931—Bias cut, black crepe dress with rhinestone clip at V neckline; deep V back; Juliet cap trimmed with rhinestones; *Excellent*; $55.

1931—Silver sequin gown; V neck; sleeveless; very form fitting; *Excellent*; $200.

1931—Ivory crepe and black satin wedding ensemble; sleeveless bias-cut long dress with rhinestone clip at square neck; fabric belt with buckle; matching clip; underslip; short bolero jacket in lace with long sleeves and rounded collar; *Mint*; $45.

1931—Mustard taffeta sleeveless evening dress; vertical fabric ruffle on each side of bodice that starts at front waistline and goes over shoulder to back waistline; rounded V-neck front, four self-fabric flowers; low V back to waist; five horizontal fabric ruffles from thigh to hem; fabric sash; *Excellent*; $45.

1931—White fox-trimmed crepe-de-chine capelet; *Excellent*; $125.

1932—Gold lace hostess gown speckled with tiny pearls; bordered with gold and blue beads; *Fair*; $250.

1933—Hot blue rayon evening dress with bolero jacket; very full short sleeves trimmed with hot pink bows; *Excellent*; $75.

1933—Emerald green sleeveless evening dress; gold metallic interwoven weighted-front scoop neckline; large gold and green velvet flower corsage effect; back has emerald pin at middle top; full-length green silk slip; full train; *Mint*; $120.

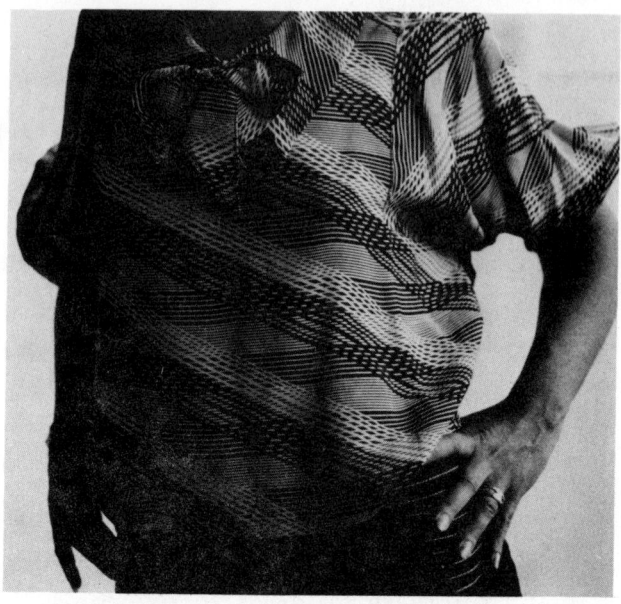

1934—Black-and-white silk blouse with dolman puffed sleeves; courtesy Early Halloween, New York City; *Excellent*; $65.

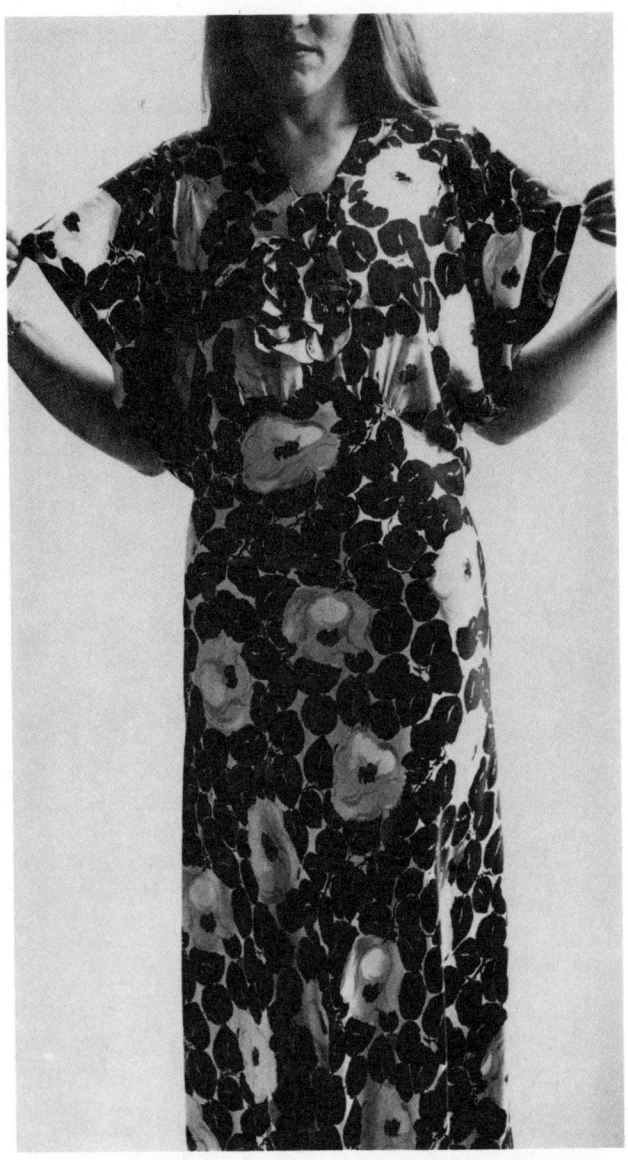

1934—Black, red, and white floral print silk-satin evening dress with short batwing sleeves; bias cut; courtesy Early Halloween, New York City; *Mint*; $250.

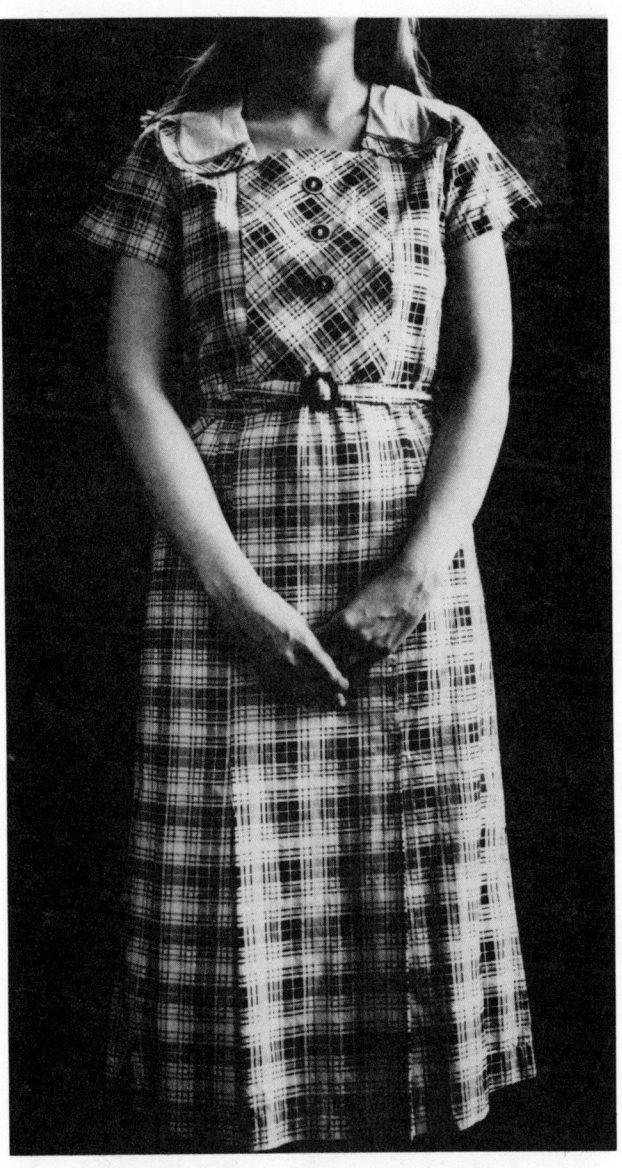

1934—Black, white, green, orange, and yellow plaid cotton dress; self belt; courtesy Early Halloween, New York City; *Excellent*; $45.

1934—Black chiffon dress with lace trim; full short sleeves with jet buttons; *Mint*; $75.

1935—Pink-and-white cotton print day dress with gored skirt; crocheted buttons; lace trim; *Mint*; $45.

1935—Floral-print silk chiffon, bias-cut skirt; matching jacket; *Excellent*; $125.

1935—Wine lace-and-net evening gown with full shoulders and fitted drop waist; *Good*; $150.

1935—Black satin and silk-crepe dress with straight skirt; long sleeves; bias-cut top; original jewelry; *Excellent*; $70.

1935—Black silk-chiffon tap-dance pants; lace inserts and pleats; *Mint*; $45.

1935—Long, pink floor-length silk-satin evening gown; plunging neckline; tiny covered buttons in back; pink fringe starts at hipline and goes to hem all around gown; *Excellent*; $95.

1935—Gold-sequined, long-sleeved net evening jacket; courtesy Early Halloween, New York City; *Mint*; $300.

1935—Salmon-and-white flowered voile Hawaiian dress; V neck; ¾-length full sleeves; five-foot train with ruffle all around bottom; *Mint*; $58.

1935—Silk-chiffon print evening dress; typical 1930s bias-cut skirt and draped bodice; courtesy Painted Lady, San Francisco; *Mint*; $100.

1936—White striped satin cocktail blouse with black satin covered buttons; taffeta and black velvet hat; courtesy Nifty 90's, Boise; *Excellent*; Blouse, $65; Hat, $25.

1936—Navy cotton dress with lace collar; ribbon belt with pewter buckle; *Excellent*; $45.

1937—Brown wool-twill suit by Adrian with striped insert and bolero effect on jacket; striped insert at pleat on skirt; courtesy Early Halloween, New York City; *Mint*; $600.

1938—White organza full-skirted long dress with leg-of-mutton-style sleeves; *Mint*; $200.

1938—Silver fox chubby jacket; black faille inserts under arms and on sides; *Good*; $200.

1938—Schiaparelli bathing suit; black velvet with rhinestone design on bodice; courtesy Early Halloween, New York City; *Mint*; $125.

1939—Beige linen dress with square neck and pockets; ecru lace on pockets and at neck; *Excellent*; $35.

1940—Beige and navy linen dress with three large buttons on each shoulder in epaulet style and with a red belt; courtesy Early Halloween, New York City; *Mint*; $100.

**1940**—Black panne-velvet top with a cobweb design in silver sequins; courtesy Early Halloween, New York City; *Excellent*; $95.

**1940**—Toast-color wool suit jacket with chocolate trim; fitted style; padded shoulders; suit pockets and peplum fully lined; label reads Lilly Anne; *Mint*; $65.

**1940**—Two-piece orchid print dress and bolero; strapless dress with split in front of skirt; boned bodice; zipper back; made and styled in Hawaii; courtesy Flamingo's, Kailua-Kona, Hawaii; *Mint*; $95.

1940—Navy-blue gabardine suit with brief scalloped cape over shoulders embroidered with carnival-glass beads; courtesy Alice Stauber, St. Louis; *Mint*; $110.

1940—Brown rayon gabardine suit, mid-calf length; fitted hip-length jacket with shoulder pads; four gray pearl buttons; patch side pockets with flaps decorated with pearl buttons; *Excellent*; $45.

1940—Gabardine western shirt; machine embroidered; padded shoulders; tailored for a woman; label reads *California Ranchwear*; *Mint*; $50.

1940—Classic black and print silk-crepe day dress; travel print in bright colors; side drape with peplum and boat neck; lettering on diagonal reads *Let's Go Somewhere*; courtesy Alice Stauber, St. Louis; *Mint*; $60.

1940—Green-and-white silk print day dress; rounded lapels; tan buttons with rhinestone centers; short cuffed sleeves; *Fair*; $16.

1940—Red silk-brocade Chinese dress with black silk pedal pushers; *Mint*; $46.

1940—Aqua sharkskin dress with caplike sleeves; full self-ruffle trim around rounded yoke and skirt; *Excellent*; $30.

1940—Red-and-white print, sheer rayon day dress; scalloped neckline trimmed with pearl-and-rhinestone flower-shaped buttons; short sleeves with little ties; *Mint*; $15.

1940—Silk day dress; emerald green with splashes of blue and pink scattered all over; 3-panel skirt with ruched pockets; black-and-gold glass buttons down front; *Fair*; $25.

1940—Knee-length white rayon gabardine dress; navy polka-dot trim on V-neck collar, on cuffs of short puffed, pleated sleeves, and down the front closing to hem; 15 star-shaped buttons; *Excellent*; $30.

1940—Turquoise crepe dress; ¾ sleeves with cuffs; fitted bodice with drop waistline, tiny knife-pleated skirt; narrow stand-up collar; *Good*; $20.

1940—Purple wool dress with padded shoulders; tan wool stripe runs from one shoulder to opposite hip; purple wool jacket with large padded shoulders; stripe on jacket runs in opposite direction to stripe on dress; *Mint*; $50.

1940—Short black velvet dress; mostly pink floral design in thick sequins at both shoulders; *Good*; $40.

1940—Day dress; beige background with tiny allover print in brown, orange, and blue; short cuffed sleeves; neat buttons down front; darts at shoulder and waistline; fabric loop trim on round neck; skirt has many gores; *Excellent*; $23.

1940—Medium brown crepe dress with padded shoulders by Baerbo; ¾ sleeves; two rhinestone pins for trim; *Mint*; $26.

1940—Black-and-mauve crepe dress; front bodice has a palm tree design in black bugle beads; ¾ sleeves; deep V neck; ¼ peplum at left hip; *Excellent*; $40.

1940—Short purple moiré evening dress; scoop neck; gathered down front; full ruffle on hip; *Mint*; $85.

1940—Crepe de chine dress with black sequins; padded shoulders; *Mint*; $85.

1940—Chartreuse dinner dress with short sleeves; squared neckline gathers into a front panel that has three scallops with clear glass buttons; straight mid-calf skirt; gathered vertical flounce decoration down left side; *Good*; $22.

1940—Hattie Carnegie navy-blue silk-tulle cocktail gown with pastel embroidered flowers all over; fitted bodice; double-circle skirt lined in navy silk; *Mint*; $275.

1940—Olive-green crepe evening dress with sequins and beads; weskit-type bodice; bias-cut skirt; *Mint*; $85.

1940—Beige silk-shantung suit blouse; *Mint*; $24.

1940—Light purple ankle-length dress with pads; cap sleeves; crystal-beaded bodice; John Jay Original; *Excellent*; $55.

1940—Blouse with padded shoulders; red and black sequins on shoulder with initials *JTI*; *Mint*; $55.

1940—One-piece mustard-color bathing suit; single tie around neck; *Good*; $8.

1940—Women's denim jeans; regular pockets; side zipper; orange stitching; straight legs; *Good*; $10.

# UNDERWEAR

1931—One-piece lounging pajamas in red-and-blue print rayon with red hip-length jacket; cuffs and pockets of jacket trimmed in same print found on the pajamas; wide bias cut on legs; courtesy Nifty 90's, Boise; *Excellent*; $65.

1931—Lounging pajamas; white silk top with green dragon design around V neckline; flared legs with inserted panels of white silk with green dragons; green silk jacket with white dragon design on sleeves and border on back; *Excellent*; $95.

1932—Dusty pink full-length wool robe; satin trim and sash; frog closure; *Excellent*; $35.

1934—Ecru silk full slip; handmade in China; appliquéd silk-crepe lace and re-embroidery; *Mint*; $150.

1934—Pink quilted-silk bed jacket; handmade in China; self buttons; peplum waist; courtesy Sweet Emaline, Atlanta; *Mint*; $75.

1934—Ecru silk full-length slip with train; handmade in China; tulle re-embroidered lace and drawn work; courtesy Sweet Emaline, Atlanta; *Mint*; $275.

1935—Burgundy satin lounging robe; high-waisted wrap to back; quilted cummerbund; bell sleeves; *Mint*; $44.

1935—White silk/cotton nightgown; triangular lace insert in hem; cut on bias; *Good*; $125.

1935—Ecru satin form-fitting slip; *Excellent*; $20.

1935—Aqua silk-satin pajamas; lace insert in bodice; courtesy Early Halloween, New York City; *Mint*; $45.

1938—Quilted silk-velvet robe; satin lining; machine-made lace collar; *Excellent*; $50.

1940—Rayon housecoat/dress with luau print incorporating Hawaiian expressions; zipper front; drop shoulder with shoulder pads; label reads *Made in Hawaii*; courtesy Flamingo's, Kailua-Kona, Hawaii; *Mint*; $75.

1940—White cotton full slip; eyelet top and ribbons; *Excellent*; $25.

1940—White seersucker nightgown; Victorian styling; tiny tucks and narrow eyelet trim on yoke; buttons down front; long sleeves; *Mint*; $15.

1940—Pale pink slip; beige lace trim at neckline and hem; *Mint*; $12.

1940—Cotton seersucker lounge dress; long with short sleeves; blue-and-white print; medium-width lapels; pocket and belt; *Fair*; $12.

1940—Quilted rayon-satin robe; full length; pale pink with multicolor floral sprays; purple lining and sash; padded shoulders; wrap closing; *Excellent*; $30.

1940—Pink quilted satin robe lined in blue silk; *Good*; $25.

1940—Two-piece satin pajama set; lace insert; *Mint*; $100.

# HATS, PURSES, SHOES, AND ACCESSORIES

1933—Cherry red fur hat; matching feathers worked into a scroll design; possibly worn by Ruby Keeler in the movie *Gold Diggers of 1933*; *Mint*; $100.

1933—Emerald-green evening pumps; label reads *I. Miller Sons/New York*; *Mint*; $40.

1934—Red straw slouch hat with red and white leather flowers; *Excellent*; $45.

1935—Lady's straw cowboy hat; wide brim; original band; Author's Collection; *Mint*; $75; *Not for sale*.

1935—White crocheted bag; wooden handle and closure; *Good*; $10.

1936—Natural straw hat; heavy, wide basketweave; grosgrain ribbon and buttons; courtesy Early Halloween, New York City; *Good*; $39.

1937—Conical hat with chiffon veil worn by Rosalind Russell in *The Women*; Private collection; courtesy Early Halloween, New York City; *Mint*; $300; *Not for sale*.

1937—Wine silk slippers with open toes; ruffled trim with high heel; courtesy Early Halloween, New York City; *Mint*; $85.

1938—Navy-blue straw hat; red velvet band; face net with red velvet dots; *Mint*; $25.

1938—Navy sequined evening hat; *Mint*; $25.

1938—Black felt hat; rhinestone clip in front; courtesy Nifty 90's, Boise; *Excellent*; $25.

1938—"Katharine Hepburn" brown-and-white saddle oxfords; courtesy Early Halloween, New York City; *Mint*; $45.

1938—Black velvet evening bag with self velvet strap; *Mint*; $20.

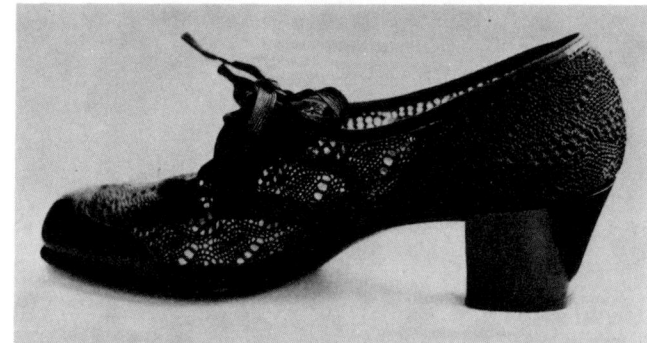

1940—Navy leather day shoes with mesh insert; courtesy Early Halloween, New York City; *Good*; $45.

1940—Brown cashmere scarf trimmed in fox; *Mint*; $40.

1940—Green felt hat with feather; *Mint*; $22.

1940—Toast-color Milano straw hat with wide ribbon; *Mint*; $25.

1940—Black Milano straw picture hat; very large brim with black grosgrain ribbon; *Mint*; $15.

# THE CARE AND CLEANING OF ANTIQUE CLOTHES

INCLUDED HERE are some very general tips for the care, cleaning, and storage of antique clothes. When you are handling or working on clothes, make sure your hands are clean and keep your work area clean. Do not smoke, eat, or drink around them and do not use writing pens of any kind. Keep the clothes away from sharp objects such as jewelry or coat hangers.

Light and air are harmful to older fabrics. I suggest a dark storage area, free from bugs and rodents, with a temperature between 65 degrees to 75 degrees. Humidity should not be over 50 percent or the clothes will mildew. A closet in one's home should fit this description.

A very important fact is that paper, cardboard boxes, and unsealed wood (like the inside of a drawer) contain acids that eat through cloth. Line drawers with acid-free tissue or unbleached muslin. Basements and attics have poor climate control and are not desirable. *Never* keep your antique clothes in direct sunlight such as in a shopwindow. *Never* keep clothes in sealed plastic bags; this creates mildew. Air should circulate around the clothes. Storing clothes flat is preferable to hanging them up because the cloth fibers can rest and there is no tension on the cloth. If you do not have flat storage space available, always use *padded* coat hangers to alleviate the tension at the shoulders of the garment. One can use regular wire hangers padded heavily with foam and then covered with an unbleached muslin sleeve. If you have a heavy skirt, use two hangers to distribute the weight.

There are several ways of cleaning antique clothes. Very fragile or old clothing should simply be aired. Such garments can be lightly vacuumed with a regular domestic cannister model turned to its lightest setting. Lay the fabric on a flat, clean, smooth surface and gently pass the vacuum over it. Contemporary or sturdier fabrics can be dry-cleaned by professional dry cleaners. Insist that fresh solvent be used. When washing white cottons one can use Woolite or Ivory Liquid or a nonionic detergent. Do not scrub but gently work the lather with your hands, rinse carefully, and press dry in a towel. Do not wring out antique clothes. Very old or historic costumes should not be pressed with a hot iron.

A source list for specialized cleaning and storage supplies as well as a bibliography of books on this subject can be found in the book *Considerations for the Care of Textiles and Costumes* by Harold F. Mailand, available from the Indianapolis Museum of Art, 1200 West 38th Street, Indianapolis, Indiana 46208.

# SOURCES FOR ANTIQUE CLOTHES

Ages Past
2803 Uter Drive
Colorado Springs, Colorado 80907

Frances Altman
1935 Peachtree Road, N.E.
Atlanta, Georgia 30309

April's Attic
197 College Street
Burlington, Vermont 05401

Best of Everything
307 East 77th Street
New York, New York 10021

Braeside Antiques
Box 765
Monmouth, Maine 04259

Campbell House Museum
1508 Locust Street
St. Louis, Missouri 63103

Club Anonymous—Vintage Clothier
284 Morewood Avenue, Shadyside
Pittsburgh, Pennsylvania 15213

Early Halloween
180 Ninth Avenue
New York, New York 10011

Estate Clothing Co.
4552 Poppleton Avenue
Omaha, Nebraska 68106

FDR Drive
109 Thompson Street
New York, New York 10012

Flamingo's
118 Kona Inn Shopping Village
75-5744 Alii Drive
Kailua-Kona, Hawaii 96740

Ginger Tree Factory
3409 Oaklawn, Suite #222
Dallas, Texas 75219

Grandpa's Barn Antiques
W. 62 N. 634 Washington Avenue
Cedarburg, Wisconsin 53012

Great Gatsby
218 North Lee Street—Old Town
Alexandria, Virginia 22314

Burnette Hurley Antiques
6720 East 32nd
Tulsa, Oklahoma 74145

Just Like Grandma's
1116 North High Street
Columbus, Ohio 43210

Laughing Cat Antiques
12703 Cutten Road
Houston, Texas 77066

Mount Vernon Antiques
Box 248
Mount Vernon, Maine 04352

Nifty 90's
1604 Front Street
Boise, Idaho 83706

Painted Lady
1838 Divisadero
San Francisco, California 94115

Puttin' on the Ritz
1639 East 19th
Eugene, Oregon 97403

Red Rose Vintage Clothes
8660 Bazaar Drive
Indianapolis, Indiana 46240

Repeat Performance
7264 Melrose Avenue
Los Angeles, California 90046

Mary Schreiter
1223 West College Avenue
Appleton, Wisconsin 54914

The Side Show
1414 Colley Avenue
Norfolk, Virginia 23507

Alice Stauber
26 Maryland Plaza
St. Louis, Missouri 63108

Sunsmith House Antiques
Route 6A, RR 2
Brewster, Massachusetts 02631

Suzi's Antiques
235 North Main Street
Farmville, Virginia 23901

Sweet Emaline
1186-A North Highland Avenue N.E.
Atlanta, Georgia 30306

Wearable Heirlooms
1028 Delta Avenue
Cincinnati, Ohio 45208